READINGS ON

DEATH OF A SALESMAN

THE GREENHAVEN PRESS

Literary Companion

TO AMERICAN LITERATURE

READINGS ON

DEATH OF A SALESMAN

Thomas Siebold, *Book Editor*

David L. Bender, *Publisher*

Bruno Leone, *Executive Editor*

Bonnie Szumski, *Series Editor*

Greenhaven Press, Inc., San Diego, CA

Every effort has been made to trace the owners of copyrighted material. The articles in this volume may have been edited for content, length, and/or reading level. The titles have been changed to enhance the editorial purpose. Those interested in locating the original source will find the complete citation on the first page of each article.

Library of Congress Cataloging-in-Publication Data

Readings on Death of a Salesman / Thomas Siebold,
    book editor.
        p.   cm. — (Greenhaven Press literary companion
    to American literature)
    Includes bibliographical references and index.
    ISBN 1-56510-839-6 (lib. bdg. : alk. paper). —
ISBN 1-56510-838-8 (pbk. : alk. paper)
    1. Miller, Arthur, 1915–   Death of a salesman.
I. Siebold, Thomas. II. Series.
PS3525. I5156D4372   1999
812'.52—dc21   98-46123
                                                                    CIP

Cover photo: Photofest

Copyright ©1999 by Greenhaven Press, Inc.
PO Box 289009
San Diego, CA 92198-9009
Printed in the U.S.A.

"Salesman *is absurdly simple!*
It's about a salesman and it's
his last day on the earth. **"**

—*Arthur Miller*

CONTENTS

Chapter 3: Relationships in *Death of a Salesman*

FOREWORD

*"'Tis the good reader that
makes the good book."*

Ralph Waldo Emerson

The story's bare facts are simple: The captain, an old and scarred seafarer, walks with a peg leg made of whale ivory. He relentlessly drives his crew to hunt the world's oceans for the great white whale that crippled him. After a long search, the ship encounters the whale and a fierce battle ensues. Finally the captain drives his harpoon into the whale, but the harpoon line catches the captain about the neck and drags him to his death.

A simple story, a straightforward plot—yet, since the 1851 publication of Herman Melville's *Moby-Dick*, readers and critics have found many meanings in the struggle between Captain Ahab and the whale. To some, the novel is a cautionary tale that depicts how Ahab's obsession with revenge leads to his insanity and death. Others believe that the whale represents the unknowable secrets of the universe and that Ahab is a tragic hero who dares to challenge fate by attempting to discover this knowledge. Perhaps Melville intended Ahab as a criticism of Americans' tendency to become involved in well-intentioned but irrational causes. Or did Melville model Ahab after himself, letting his fictional character express his anger at what he perceived as a cruel and distant god?

Although literary critics disagree over the meaning of *Moby-Dick*, readers do not need to choose one particular interpretation in order to gain an understanding of Melville's novel. Instead, by examining various analyses, they can gain numerous insights into the issues that lie under the surface of the basic plot. Studying the writings of literary critics can also aid readers in making their own assessments of *Moby-Dick* and other literary works and in developing analytical thinking skills.

The Greenhaven Literary Companion Series was created with these goals in mind. Designed for young adults, this unique anthology series provides an engaging and comprehensive introduction to literary analysis and criticism. The essays included in the Literary Companion Series are chosen for their accessibility to a young adult audience and are expertly edited in consideration of both the reading and comprehension levels of this audience. In addition, each essay is introduced by a concise summation that presents the contributing writer's main themes and insights. Every anthology in the Literary Companion Series contains a varied selection of critical essays that cover a wide time span and express diverse views. Wherever possible, primary sources are represented through excerpts from authors' notebooks, letters, and journals and through contemporary criticism.

Each title in the Literary Companion Series pays careful consideration to the historical context of the particular author or literary work. In-depth biographies and detailed chronologies reveal important aspects of authors' lives and emphasize the historical events and social milieu that influenced their writings. To facilitate further research, every anthology includes primary and secondary source bibliographies of articles and/or books selected for their suitability for young adults. These engaging features make the Greenhaven Literary Companion series ideal for introducing students to literary analysis in the classroom or as a library resource for young adults researching the world's great authors and literature.

Exceptional in its focus on young adults, the Greenhaven Literary Companion Series strives to present literary criticism in a compelling and accessible format. Every title in the series is intended to spark readers' interest in leading American and world authors, to help them broaden their understanding of literature, and to encourage them to formulate their own analyses of the literary works that they read. It is the editors' hope that young adult readers will find these anthologies to be true companions in their study of literature.

INTRODUCTION

Considered an artistic triumph by most critics, *Death of a Salesman* brought Arthur Miller celebrity, a comfortable living, and recognition as an accomplished dramatist. The play's humor, sympathy, and sense of modern tragedy made its main figure, Willy Loman, an American everyman. Willy, his two sons, and his bewildered wife touch a nerve in the American psyche. Audiences see themselves or somebody they know in Willy as he tries unsuccessfully to cope with a modern materialistic society driven by an unrelenting and seemingly unforgiving success ethic. Structuring his play expressionistically, Miller broke down the conventional restraints of time and place, moving the audience into Willy's past as events of the present triggered memories. Miller wrote in his autobiography that "the moving in and out of the present had to be not simply indicative but a tactile transformation that the audience could feel as well as comprehend, and indeed come to dread as returning memory threatens to bring Willy closer to his end." In short, the experience of the play carries the audience into the head of Willy to feel both intellectually and viscerally his loneliness, his needs, and his struggle to leave a mark on this world.

Since its first public staging at the Locust Street Theatre in Philadelphia, *Death of a Salesman* established Arthur Miller as an important and, at times, controversial figure of twentieth-century dramatic history. The play has generated volumes of critical debate: Some drama critics dispute the play's status as a tragedy since it does not fit traditional guidelines for tragedy; some attack the play for not being intellectual; others argue that the play is sentimental and naive; and many challenge Miller's view of capitalism. No matter what the criticism, *Death of a Salesman* has had a profound effect on audiences around the world, often moving them to tears. Reflecting on the play's extremely successful production in Beijing, China, Arthur Miller summed up the experience by stating that "Willy was representative everywhere, in every kind of system, of ourselves in this time."

Readings on Death of a Salesman is designed to help students gain a greater appreciation of Arthur Miller's greatest dramatic achievement. The carefully edited articles provide an overview of the play's themes, characterization, structure, philosophy, and impact on American theater. Each of the literary essays is readable, manageable in length, and focuses on concepts suitable for a beginning exploration into the genre of literary criticism. Additionally, this diverse overview of *Death of a Salesman* presents students with a wealth of material for writing reports, designing oral presentations, or enriching their understanding of drama as art.

ARTHUR MILLER: A BIOGRAPHY

The major turning point in Arthur Miller's career occurred when his most critically celebrated play, *Death of a Salesman*, opened on Broadway in February 1949. The production of *Death of a Salesman* transformed Miller's life. The play won the Pulitzer Prize, the Antoinette Perry (Tony) Award, and the Drama Critics' Circle Award. Its success brought Miller fame, critical praise, and substantial wealth. Heralded as one of America's most promising young playwrights, Miller secured his fame after more than ten years of artistic struggle.

Few artists achieve their goals as substantially as Arthur Miller did. But despite his success, Miller continues to question his achievements. His concern for the common man and his distrust of society's institutions often make him feel guilty and uncomfortable with his celebrity. He fears that he will no longer be able to write about the poor when he himself is rich, or that perhaps the trappings of fame will separate him from the essential feelings and insights that generated a play like *Death of a Salesman*. In his autobiography, *Timebends: A Life*, Miller writes, "I was not the first to experience the guilt of success (which, incidentally, was reinforced by leftist egalitarian convictions), and though I suspected the truth, I was unable to do much about it." For Arthur Miller, the struggle to write is a struggle to learn about himself, understand his role as a writer in society, and maintain his idealism, integrity, and political views against popular opinion and criticism.

MILLER'S CHILDHOOD

Born on October 17, 1915, in New York City, Arthur Asher Miller grew up in a middle-class household on 112th Street in Manhattan with his older brother, Kermit, younger sister, Joan, and parents, Isidore and Augusta Miller. His father, an Austrian immigrant, was, for most of Arthur's youth, a successful manufacturer of ladies' coats. Isidore, like many practical-minded immigrant Jews, entered the garment business when he came to New York City in the late 1800s. Arthur's mother, a school-teacher before she married Isidore, was a conscientious parent who taught her children the customs and heritage of Judaism. Augusta was an avid reader who, according to Miller, could begin a book in the afternoon, finish it by midnight, and recall its details years later. Since no one in the family but Augusta was a reader, she hired a Columbia University student for two dollars a week to discuss novels with her. Augusta was a bright, sensitive woman who was pressed by Miller's grandfathers into marriage within months of graduating with honors from high school. When she told her children the story of her arranged marriage, Miller remembers that her look would suddenly "blacken as she clenched her jaws in anger. 'Like a cow!' she would mutter." In *Timebends: A Life*, Miller suggests that his mother was a "woman haunted by a world she could not reach out to, by books she would not get to read, concerts she would not get to attend, and above all, interesting people she'd never get to meet."

Arthur lived a comfortable middle-class life until age fourteen. It was at this time, in the early stages of the Great Depression, that the family's garment business failed. The loss of the business in 1928 put a great strain on the Millers: Isidore became depressed, both Kermit and Arthur had to take jobs, and the family was forced to move out of their house. As an adolescent, Arthur was deeply disappointed by his father's inability to cope with the loss: "My father simply went more deeply silent, and his naps grew longer, and his mouth seemed to dry up. I could not avoid awareness of my mother's anger at his waning powers." Arthur was also disillusioned with the economic system that put his family in their new predicament; he grew suspicious of the powers that controlled the wealth and the social machinery of society. Later Miller wrote that the depression made him aware that life was often a struggle against powerful social forces outside of the family.

With the loss of their business, the Millers moved to Brooklyn to be near relatives. Arthur attended James Madison High School, where he was actively involved in football and other sports, not unlike Biff Loman in *Death of a Salesman*. Miller focused on staying in good physical shape and improving his athletic skills, not his studies. His friends were athletes, not intellectuals.

After high school, Miller applied to the University of Michigan, but was rejected because his grades were too low.

To earn money, he took odd jobs, including a brief stint in the garment business doing various low-level tasks. It was here that he witnessed firsthand how salesmen were often brusquely dismissed or ordered about by insensitive buyers and employers. Later, of course, Miller would create the most famous salesman in literature, Willy Loman. In 1932 Miller began to read simply to occupy his mind between jobs. He read voraciously, particularly Russian writers Fyodor Dostoyevsky and Leo Tolstoy. His discovery of the power of literature sparked his dream of becoming a writer.

MILLER'S COLLEGE YEARS

After several rejected applications, Miller was finally admitted to the University of Michigan in 1934, where he studied journalism, economics, and history. His broad range of study made him skeptical that any one discipline or institution had a monopoly on truth. As a sensitive young college student, Miller began a quest to understand how society changed, how it influenced the individual, and how it could be improved. Miller was attracted to the ideals of socialism—especially its concern for the rights and dignity of the common person. Exhilarated by the prospect of a new social order built on reason, Miller and his fellow student socialists expected "a socialist evolution of the planet" that would bestow a "new and just system." Although his enthusiasm for socialism eventually diminished, many of the liberal political and social ideals he formed in college stayed with him throughout his writing career.

In his junior year, Miller entered a college playwriting contest and, to his surprise, won the first prize of $250. His play *No Villain*, whose characters are modeled on Miller's own family members, deals with the tension within a garment manufacturing family during a bitter labor strike. In *No Villain*, Miller introduces many of the themes and conflicts that dominate his later and more artistic works: the tension between selfishness and humanitarianism, class struggle, conflicts between family members, and the healing bond of family loyalty. Encouraged by the praise of *No Villain*, Miller decided to dedicate himself to writing drama.

Miller graduated from college in 1938 with a degree in English and subsequently supported himself by writing for the Federal Theater Project, a government-sponsored program promoting American writers. While with the project, Miller and fellow Michigan graduate Norman Rosten coauthored *Lis-*

ten My Children, an uninspired comedy. The Federal Theater Project did not last long, however: The recently established House Un-American Activities Committee (HUAC) suspected the program of infiltration by Communists and abolished it. With the project closed, Miller not only lost his twenty-two-dollar weekly salary, he was also introduced to the harsh tactics of HUAC. Sixteen years later, in 1956, Miller encountered HUAC again when the committee suspected him of subversive behavior and subpoenaed him to defend his social and political views.

MILLER'S EARLY WORK

In 1940 Miller married his sweetheart from the University of Michigan, Mary Slattery. Mary, daughter of an insurance salesman, was a bright student who, according to Miller, had more faith in his ability to write than he had himself. Although she was not actively religious, she was reared a Catholic, and at the time of their marriage both sets of parents were concerned about the intermarriage of a Jew and a gentile. Although the religious conflict in their extended family was disconcerting, Miller and his young wife believed that they could rise above the "parochial narrowness of mind, prejudices, racism, and the irrational" that they felt the tension represented. The couple had two children, Robert and Jane. During World War II, Mary worked as a secretary and Arthur, unable to participate in military service because of a nagging football injury, worked on ships in the Brooklyn Navy Yard and wrote radio plays for the Columbia Broadcasting System. Despite the fact that script writing turned out to be rather lucrative (approximately one hundred dollars a script), Miller hated writing for radio; he chafed under the restrictions and limitations imposed by the radio networks and advertisers and became increasingly suspicious of mixing commercialism and the arts. Nevertheless, as the radio scripts demanded crisp writing and tight organization, this work helped the young playwright refine his craft.

Miller received his first theatrical break in 1944 when *The Man Who Had All the Luck* was staged on Broadway. The play explores the roles of fate, luck, success, and failure in one's life. Unfortunately, it was not well received by critics and closed after only six performances. In his autobiography Miller says of this play that "standing at the back of the house during the single performance I could bear to watch, I could blame nobody. All I knew was that the whole thing was a well-meant botch,

like music played on the wrong instruments in a false scale."
Although this play and his other early dramas were unsuccessful, Miller was learning what it took to write a meaningful
play. He developed an ear for dialogue and he learned the craft
of staging dramas, the needs of actors, and the demands of an
audience. Success was not far away.

The Man Who Had All the Luck lost a great deal of money
and Miller, now in debt, felt pressured to write his next project, a novel entitled *Focus.* The story's main character is a
non-Jew named Lawrence Newman who, after he begins to
wear glasses, is mistaken for a Jew. Lawrence is shocked and
outraged when he encounters senseless prejudice and anti-
Semitism. The novel met with moderate success and was published in England, France, Germany, and Italy. As a Jew himself, Miller experienced only limited encounters with
anti-Semitism as a child, but once he began working after high
school he was shocked at the extent and intensity of anti-
Semitism in America. Because of his own anti-Semitic experiences and following revelations of the Holocaust, Miller committed himself to a lifelong fight opposing anti-Semitism.

MILLER'S FIRST DRAMATIC SUCCESS

At age thirty a frustrated Miller, faced with meager respect
and success as a dramatist, decided to give playwriting one
last try. Based on an incidental comment by his wife's mother
about a young girl who turned in her father to the FBI for
manufacturing faulty aircraft parts, Miller began a two-year
task of diligently writing and rewriting the play *All My Sons.*
He had decided that if he was going to fail as a writer, he
would go out with the best possible script. In 1947 this realistic social drama was coproduced by stage and film director
Elia Kazan, who at the time was well known but not yet famous. Kazan helped Miller focus and polish the work.

All My Sons follows a thematic pattern Miller established
in *Focus.* As the play opens, the audience perceives an at-
mosphere of normality, a world that is calm, orderly, and
peaceful. This placid world is disrupted as the play pro-
gresses and the characters expose the audience to a world of
tension and disillusionment. The intent of the play is to reveal truths about family, moral decision making, and the role
of the individual in society. Although it received mixed reviews, *All My Sons* was widely popular with theatergoers and
enjoyed a profitable run of 328 performances. It won the
Drama Critics' Circle Award and provided Miller with the re-

newed energy and resources to press on in his career. On the heels of its Broadway success, in 1948 *All My Sons* was made into a movie starring Edward G. Robinson and Burt Lancaster.

Reflecting on this period of his life, Miller recalls conflicting emotions. On one hand he was proud of his success, but on the other hand he experienced some awkwardness: "As a success I was occasionally greeted by people on the street with a glazed expression that was pleasant but made me feel unnervingly artificial. My identification with life's failures was being menaced by my fame." Miller's reactions aside, with *All My Sons* his status as a playwright was established.

MILLER'S MASTER DRAMA

With the money he earned from *All My Sons*, Miller bought a modest farm in Roxbury, Connecticut. On a knoll by the woods, Miller built a small cabin where he escaped and wrote undisturbed. He notes that while construction was going on at the cabin, he had thought of two lines for his next play, based on a salesman he had known when he worked for his father: "Willy!" and "It's all right. I came back." Miller also knew that he would use the name Loman, a name that suddenly came to him one evening as he was randomly jotting down notes. The name is based on a character, Lohmann, that Miller had seen years earlier in Fritz Lang's film *The Testament of Dr. Mabuse*. The movie and the name stuck in the playwright's mind, evoking for Miller an image of "a terror-stricken man calling into the void for help that will never come."

Early one morning, sitting in his completed studio, Miller started writing; by the next morning, he had written half a play, which he called *Inside Your Head*. In his autobiography, Miller recalls the condition he was in when he finally stopped writing: "I realized that I had been weeping—my eyes still burned and my throat was sore from talking it all out and shouting and laughing. I would be stiff when I woke, aching as if I had played four hours of football or tennis and now had to face the start of another game." The second half of the play took just six weeks to complete. As he looks back on the creative process, Miller suggests that he never felt like he wrote the play, rather the play just "happened." Producers Walter Fried and Kermit Bloomgarden liked the play immediately and convinced Elia Kazan to direct it. When Kazan called Miller to tell him that he loved the work, Kazan broke off in mid-sentence and, like many who have read or seen the play, was overcome with sadness because he recognized his father in Willy. Kazan knew that it could be a great play. With extensive rewriting, the play opened in January 1949 with a new name—*Death of a Salesman.*

Death of a Salesman premiered in Philadelphia to glowing reviews. Years later, Miller told of his experience watching the first performance. At the play's end the audience did not applaud. Instead, they sat in stunned silence, stood up, put their coats on, and sat down again, not wanting to leave the theater. Some people were crying. Finally, almost as an afterthought, the applause exploded. From Philadelphia the production moved to the Morosco Theater on Broadway, where it played to packed houses and overwhelming approval. Driving home from the Morosco premiere at three in the morning, Miller and his wife, Mary, sat in silence, realizing that life would never be the same again. In *Timebends,* Miller writes that they both felt anxious, unaware that "the aphrodisiac of celebrity, still nameless, came and sat between us in the car." *Death of a Salesman* ran for 742 performances before it closed on November 18, 1950, having won the Drama Critics' Circle Award and the Pulitzer Prize.

The play created a strong response wherever it was staged. Audiences were often emotionally unnerved, right wing conservatives saw it as an attack on capitalism or an expression of moral decadence, liberals endorsed it as prosocialist, and critics debated how to categorize it. Miller himself was startled at the devastating sadness that the play often generated in the audience. In the introduction to *The Collected Plays,* Miller suggests that he often felt embarrassed as he watched the tears flow from the eyes of the audience, feeling that he was somehow reinforcing the notion that life was not worth living. The playwright considers himself an optimist who wrote the play half in joy and who states bluntly that "I am convinced the play is not a document of pessimism, a philosophy in which I do not believe."

With *Death of a Salesman,* Miller became famous and again he struggled with the notion of success. Reflecting on the glory of the first night after the New York opening, with rave reviews flowing from all the critics, Miller writes, "I had striven all my life to win this night, and it was here, and I was this celebrated man who had amazingly little to do with me, or I with him. . . . My dreams of many years had become too damned real, and the reality was less than the dream."

POLITICAL ACTIVITY AND *THE CRUCIBLE*

In the late 1940s and into the 1950s, the cold war between the Soviet Union and the United States, accompanied by a super-power arms race, created an international mood of suspicion and fear. Political, social, and business leaders were increasingly concerned that communism threatened the American "way of life." This so-called Red Scare often bordered on paranoia. It was a tense era, when federal workers were required to take loyalty oaths to pledge their allegiance to America and the government established loyalty boards to investigate reports of Communist sympathizers. In 1950 Wisconsin senator Joseph McCarthy and the House Un-American Activities Committee, established to uncover subversive infiltration into American life, turned their anti-Communist attention to Hollywood and the intellectual community.

In April 1952, HUAC called Miller's director, Elia Kazan, to testify about Communist activity in the theater and motion-picture business. He was asked to name individuals whom he knew had been members of Communist groups, and Kazan named Miller. Both Kazan and Miller were liberals, who, like many intellectuals and artists, dabbled with leftist ideas and causes. Arthur Miller had attended a few meetings of Communist Writers of New York, had signed a petition that protested the banning of the Communist Party, and had been named in a 1947 issue of the *Daily Worker*, a socialist newspaper. Moreover, during the war years, Miller was intrigued by Marxism and had attended some Marxist study courses. Because of his economic troubles during the depression, Miller felt he had experienced the Marxist struggle of the worker against the employer. In *Timebends: A Life* Miller writes that "the concept of a classless society had a disarming sweetness that called forth the generosity of youth. The true condition of man, it seemed, was the complete opposite of the competitive system that I had assumed was normal, with all its mutual hatreds and conniving." But despite the fact that Miller supported left-wing causes, he was not a Communist Party member or sympathizer. After Kazan, HUAC targeted Miller.

Miller was finally subpoenaed to appear before HUAC in 1956. Unlike his friend Kazan, Miller refused to name names. The committee members were unimpressed with the playwright's explanation of artistic freedom and cited Miller for contempt of Congress. Although Miller was found guilty by an overwhelming vote of 373 to 9, public support for his openness and honesty resulted in a reconsideration of his case. In 1958 the U.S. Court of Appeals for the District of Columbia reversed Miller's conviction, stating that he was not informed adequately of the risks involved in incurring contempt.

Miller's response to this anti-Communist fear, guilt, and hysteria was *The Crucible.* In 1951 Miller read Marion Starkey's book *The Devil in Massachusetts* which details the strange events of the Salem witchcraft trials. Despite the dramatic possibilities of the topic, Miller initially rejected the idea of writing a play on the subject, believing that his own sense of rationality would not allow him to capture the wild irrationality of the events. In his autobiography the playwright writes why he changed his mind, "gradually, over weeks, a living connection between myself and Salem, and between Salem and Washington, was made in my mind—for whatever else they might be, I saw that the hearings in Washington were profoundly and even avowedly ritualistic." Although he had been introduced to the witchcraft trials in his American history class at Michigan, Miller decided to travel to the Historical Society of Salem in order to read firsthand accounts of the phenomenon. Ironically, the day before he left for Salem, Elia Kazan phoned to say that he had agreed to cooperate with HUAC.

At the Salem courthouse Miller studied the town records of 1692. He found that initially the dialect of the interrogations sounded gnarled and he mouthed the words out loud until he "came to love its feel, like burnished wood." In the evenings he walked through the town trying to capture the mood of the period. In his "Introduction" to the *Collected Plays* Miller writes that the lunacy of McCarthyism and the terror of Salem began to merge into a central image that would carry his play, "above all, above all horrors, I saw accepted the notion that conscience was no longer a private matter but one of state administration. I saw men handing conscience to other men and thanking other men for the opportunity of doing so."

The Crucible took Miller almost one year to write. The mood of the country remained tense. According to Miller, the average citizen was willing to accept insanity as routine. In *Timebends: A Life* the playwright exemplifies this mood by recalling the fate of "The Hook," Miller's screenplay about union corruption written in 1951. The head of Columbia Pictures, Harry Cohn, after showing the script to the FBI, wanted Miller to change the gangsters to Communists. When Miller refused, he was chastised by Cohn, "The minute we try to make the script pro-American you pull out." Because of this type of harassment, Miller knew that it would take a great deal of courage for Kermit Bloomgarden to produce *The Crucible* on Broadway. Indeed, the momentum working against Miller was building: In Peoria, Illinois, the American Legion and the Jaycees gained publicity by leading a successful boycott of *Death of a Salesman,* and the Catholic War Veterans had persuaded the army to ban its theatrical groups from staging any Miller play. Nevertheless, *The Crucible* opened on Broadway in 1953 for a decent run of 197 performances. The staging received mixed reviews, but what disappointed the author more than the critical reception of the play was the hostility of the audience. In *Timebends: A Life* Miller writes that "as the theme of the play was revealed, an invisible sheet of ice formed over their heads, thick enough to skate on. In the lobby at the end, people with whom I had some fairly close professional acquaintanceships passed me by as though I were invisible."

As the Red Scare waned, the popularity of *The Crucible* grew. The play had a very successful off-Broadway production in 1954, 1956, and 1965; it was dramatized on television with George C. Scott as John Proctor; and today it is Miller's most frequently produced play, staged every week somewhere in the world for forty-odd years. The Bantam and Penguin editions of *The Crucible* have sold more than 6 million copies. Modern audiences, long past the McCarthy paranoia, enjoy the universal themes that the drama embodies.

In 1996, when Miller was 81, his screenplay of *The Crucible* was released with Daniel Day-Lewis as John Proctor, Joan Allen as Elizabeth, Winona Ryder as Abigail, and Paul Scofield as Judge Danforth. Enjoying the critical success of the movie, Miller looked back on the evolution of the play in an article in the *New Yorker.* He argues that he wrote the play out of desperation, "motivated in some great part by the paralysis that had set in among many liberals who, despite their discomfort with the inquisitors' violations of civil rights, were fearful, and with good reason, of being identified as covert Communists if they should protest too strongly." Although the elderly playwright isn't exactly sure what *The Crucible* is saying to people today, he is confident "that its paranoid center is still pumping out the same darkly attractive warning that it did in the fifties."

MILLER'S LIFE WITH MARILYN MONROE

By 1951 Mary and Arthur's marriage was beginning to deteriorate, perhaps under the demands of a successful writing career or the pressures of celebrity, or perhaps because Elia Kazan had by then introduced Miller to Marilyn Monroe. Miller comments in *Timebends: A Life* that "when we shook hands the shock of her body's motion sped through me, a sensation at odds with her sadness amid all this glamour and technology." At one point Miller characterized the actress as "the golden girl who was like champagne on the screen." Although they had an occasional correspondence, they did not pursue a serious relationship until 1954, when Monroe divorced her husband Joe DiMaggio, one of the most famous baseball players of his era, and moved to New York City.

The next two years were tumultuous for Arthur Miller. In September 1955 two of Miller's one-act plays, *A View from the Bridge* and *A Memory of Two Mondays*, opened at the Coronet Theater in New York to disappointing and discouraging reviews. In June of that year Miller had contracted with the New York City Youth Board to write a screenplay, but when the project was announced reporter Frederick Woltman viciously attacked Miller for his leftist political views in the *New York Herald-Tribune*. The newspaper article and pressure from the paper's management forced the Youth Board to cancel Miller's film project.

In the early months of 1956, Miller divorced Mary Grace Slattery. Soon after the divorce, in the midst of his political battles with HUAC, Miller made the surprise announcement that he and Marilyn Monroe had been secretly married in a Jewish ceremony (only seventeen days after his divorce). Marilyn had just completed filming the movie *Bus Stop*, and, troubled by personal problems, looked forward to a stable life with Miller. The newspapers minutely and voraciously scrutinized the marriage. Marilyn was depicted as a volatile, sexy bombshell and Miller was pictured as a self-sufficient, intellectual writer. The contrast in personalities, the publicity, and the pressures that both were feeling at the time virtually guaranteed that the marriage would suffer.

Throughout the course of their marriage, Miller's writing fell into a slump. Life with Marilyn consumed him; her need for attention, her mood swings, and her reliance on alcohol and drugs required inordinate amounts of Miller's energy. Miller did manage to adapt his short story "The Misfits," which was first published in *Esquire* in 1957, into a screenplay specifically for Marilyn. The movie *The Misfits*, directed by John Huston, was filmed in Nevada with Montgomery Clift, Clark Gable, and Marilyn in the pivotal role of Roslyn.

During the filming, Marilyn, haunted by depression and drugs, broke down and required time to recuperate in the hospital. By this time the marriage was close to failure. In his autobiography Miller states that Marilyn, confused about who she was, "wanted everything, but one thing contradicted another; physical admiration threatened to devalue her person, yet she became anxious if her appearance was ignored."

The Misfits was first released in 1961 and met with moderate success. That year Marilyn filed for a Mexican divorce and Miller's mother died. For the next twelve months, Miller kept a low profile, publishing only two short stories, "Please Don't Kill Anything" and "The Prophecy." When Marilyn committed suicide with an overdose of sleeping pills in 1962, Miller refused to attend her funeral because he believed the publicity would turn her tragedy into a "circus." The playwright remained silent.

MILLER IN THE 1960s

During the filming of *The Misfits*, Miller met the woman who would become his third wife, Ingeborg (Inge) Morath. Inge, a Vienna-born photographer, was on the film set to take rehearsal photographs. The daughter of research chemists, Inge was educated in Berlin and worked for a while as the Austrian bureau chief for the magazine *Heute*. Both Marilyn and Arthur liked Inge. Miller was immediately attracted to her independence, her strength of character, and her talent as a photographer. Marilyn Monroe also gravitated to her because of the photographer's kindness and nonaggressive attitude. Marilyn particularly appreciated the fact that Inge portrayed her with great affection and sensitivity. At a time when Miller was obsessed with his failing marriage and his stalled writing career, Inge's confidence and stability must have been very appealing.

Despite Miller's resolve never to marry again, just over a year after his divorce from Monroe, Miller and Morath married in February 1962, six months before Monroe's suicide on August 5. Arthur and Inge would have a daughter, Rebecca, eighteen months later. Miller was extremely happy with Inge, but he was struggling to find the inspiration to write again. The Millers spent most of their time at Roxbury. Here, Miller worked on his next play, *After the Fall*, his first in nine years. *After the Fall* opened in 1964 at the ANTA Theater–Washington Square. Swamped by preproduction publicity, the play was hyped in the media as not only the reemergence of a great playwright but also a play about Marilyn Monroe. *After the Fall* suffered some of the worst criticism that Miller had ever received. Many critics accused Miller of overusing obvious autobiographical details and shamelessly exploiting his relationship with the popular actress. The main character, Quentin, appears to be Miller himself and the character Maggie, who dies of an overdose of sleeping pills, recalls the recently deceased Monroe. Miller argues that the harsh criticism was inevitable: "I was soon widely hated, but the play had spoken the truth as, after all, it was obliged to do, and if the truth was clothed in pain, perhaps it was important for the audience to confront it uncomfortably and even in the anger of denial." *After the Fall* incorporates the despair of *The Misfits* and contains some of the familiar Miller themes of guilt, self-deception, and the quest for meaning.

Despite the controversy, *After the Fall* played to large audiences and Miller was encouraged by his producers to write another. His new play, *Incident at Vichy*, was written in a very short time and opened in 1964, again to reviews that were generally unfavorable. Based on the story of an analyst friend, Dr. Rudolph Loewenstein, who hid from the Nazis in Vichy France in 1942, the play attacks anti-Semitism. Interestingly, *Incident at Vichy* was not produced in France because of the fear that audiences might resent the implication that the French cooperated with the Nazi attack on the Jews.

MILLER'S FIGHT FOR ARTISTIC FREEDOM

In the mid-1960s Miller's plays were often staged before large audiences in Europe, where the playwright was very popular. As a result, Miller spent a good deal of time in Europe viewing and helping present his work. While in Paris in 1965, Miller was encouraged to become the next president of PEN, an international writers' organization of poets, playwrights, editors, essayists, and novelists. PEN was established after World War I by writers including George Bernard Shaw and H.G. Wells to help fight censorship and champion the freedom of writers. Miller was skeptical at first, but after a few days of reflection he agreed to serve as its new leader. Having accepted the responsibility of the PEN presidency, he realized that "willy-nilly, I was pitched into the still indeterminate tangle of detente politics to begin a new and totally unexpected stage of my learning life."

As the head of PEN for the next four years, Miller dedicated himself to uplifting the social and political status of writers.

Miller believed that PEN must serve as the conscience of the world's writing community. Perhaps his dedication to this task stemmed from his treatment by HUAC, where the playwright learned firsthand that writers are often trapped by political pressures. As did many organizations after World War II, PEN operated with a cold war mentality that made it uncompromisingly anti-Soviet. In the sixties, as relations with Eastern Europe were being reexamined, PEN was finally making some attempts to enlist and support Soviet writers. As president, Miller convinced a Soviet delegation, headed by the Russian writer Alexei Surkov, to join the international organization.

Miller's dedication to PEN and the writers it represented is exemplified by the fact that Miller delivered a scheduled speech at the opening of the New York PEN Congress in 1966 despite the fact that his father died that day. Miller found the strength to deliver the speech because he was convinced that PEN was the one organization that could apply leverage to protect the rights of writers internationally. Before he retired as PEN president in 1969, Miller urged governments around the world to release writers who were imprisoned for political reasons, particularly in Lithuania, South Africa, Czechoslovakia, Latin America, and the Soviet Union.

In 1968 Miller resumed playwriting with *The Price*, a work about two brothers who cannot overcome their anger with each other. Reminiscent of his earlier work, *The Price* probes family relationships, suffocating illusions, and the power of the past to influence the present. The original staging of the play was beset by problems that troubled Miller. The director and actors were caught in a battle of artistic and egotistical differences, the lead performer dropped out because of illness, and the playwright himself was eventually enlisted to direct the play during the week before it opened on Broadway at the Morosco Theater. Despite its problems, the play opened to cordial but generally unenthusiastic reviews and ran for 425 performances. At the same time *The Price* opened, Viking Press, Miller's publisher, awarded the playwright a gold title page of *Death of a Salesman* to honor the sale of 1 million copies. This honor emphasizes the fact that despite the mixed reviews that Miller often received, his audience deeply appreciates the power of his work.

MILLER'S POLITICAL ACTIVISM

Professionally rejuvenated by the success of *The Price*, Miller carried his influence into the arena of politics. Dismayed by the

1963 assassination of President John F. Kennedy, racial inequality, poverty, and the escalating U.S. involvement in Vietnam, Miller accepted the nomination by his fellow Roxbury, Connecticut, Democrats to attend the 1968 Chicago Democratic National Convention as their delegate. Miller went to Chicago to support peace activist Eugene McCarthy and to introduce a resolution on the floor of the convention to cease U.S. bombing in Vietnam. When his resolution was rejected, Miller wrote that he "felt totally defeated by the absence of any spoken word commemorating the long fight to end the war, and by the abdication of the men who had led the struggle within the Democratic Party and were now allowing it to vanish . . . unmourned and unsung." The convention itself turned chaotic and the antiwar protests outside the convention hall turned violent as the Chicago police clashed with protesters. This experience seemed to cap Miller's fear that values in America were breaking down, violence was becoming epidemic, and government was acting with increased paranoia and force.

Reflecting on his political activism in *Timebends: A Life*, the playwright states that "the sixties was a time of stalemate for me. . . . I could find no refreshing current of history such as I had imagined touching in the thirties and forties, only a moral stagnation that mocked creation itself." Nevertheless, Miller reaffirmed his need to write social drama because, despite the chaos of the age, the common people "still wanted better lives for their kids, wished marriages could last, and clung to a certain biological decency."

MILLER IN THE 1970S

In the 1970s Miller wrote three plays: *The Creation of the World and Other Business* (1972), *The American Clock* (1976), and *The Archbishop's Ceiling* (1977). The productions of all three works were harshly criticized. *The Creation of the World and Other Business* closed after only twenty performances; *The Archbishop's Ceiling* had a short life at Washington's Kennedy Center. However, like a delayed reaction, both *The American Clock* and *The Archbishop's Ceiling* found a receptive audience in London during the mid-1980s.

Throughout the 1970s Miller continued to fight tirelessly for the rights of individuals and the freedom of writers. For example, he helped free Brazilian writer Augusto Boal, imprisoned for his political beliefs. In 1972 Miller publicly criticized the three-year sentence given to publisher Ralph Ginzburg for an obscenity conviction that was appealed all the way to the

U.S. Supreme Court. Because of a letter to Miller from famous Czech poet and playwright Pavel Kohout, Miller organized fifty-three other writers and literary figures to sign a written statement sent to the Czech leaders protesting their arrest of dissident thinkers. Miller was a major voice in the process to free dissident Russian writer Aleksandr Solzhenitsyn, whose moral strength Miller had compared to that of John Proctor in *The Crucible.* For his effort, the Soviet government banned all of Miller's works. The irony was not lost on Miller, who pointed out that his plays had been under attack by his own government for his suspected Communist sympathies and that now the Soviet government had banned his work for pushing American-style individual rights.

Perhaps the best example of Miller's involvement in the struggle of the individual against governmental authority is found in the case of Peter Reilly, who was convicted of brutally slashing his mother's throat in Canaan, Connecticut, in 1973. The case came to Miller's attention two years later when he read the transcript of Reilly's interrogation. Miller, like the friends and neighbors of the Reilly family, felt that the police had methodically and cynically broken the will of the exhausted and frightened young Peter and forced him to sign a confession. Miller enlisted the help of a lawyer friend and a private investigator to reopen the case, bring about a new trial, and ultimately free Peter Reilly. The Reilly case was a perfect cause for the playwright who had for so long concerned himself with individual rights, the abuse of authority, the perplexing nature of truth, and the themes of justice and morality. The Reilly case also reflects Miller's fascination with the law. To the playwright, who includes a lawyer in almost all of his plays, the law is the last defense against society's inability to see or accept the truth. Reflecting on the case in his autobiography, Miller writes, "If the long months of the Reilly case left a darkened picture of man, it was no less perplexing for being accompanied by the most unlikely examples of courage and goodness, of people rising to the occasion when there was little reason to expect they would."

MILLER'S REVIVAL IN THE 1980s

During the eighties Arthur Miller's works experienced a worldwide revival. Shortly after *A View from the Bridge* opened on Broadway in 1983, Miller and his wife traveled to Beijing, China, to see a production of *Death of a Salesman.* In Beijing the audience responded positively to the elementary human concerns dramatically portrayed in *Death of a Salesman*. Miller writes in his autobiography that "the Chinese reaction to my Beijing production of *Salesman* would confirm what had become more and more obvious over the decades in the play's hundreds of productions throughout the world: Willy was representative everywhere, in every kind of system, of ourselves in this time."

In 1984 the revival continued on Broadway with the opening of *Death of a Salesman* starring Dustin Hoffman as Willy Loman. Dustin Hoffman also played the lead in the 1985 CBS televised production of the play, which was broadcast to an audience of more than 25 million viewers. In addition, *The Price* was successfully revived on Broadway and in 1989 *The Crucible*, directed by Arvin Brown, was staged in New Haven. America was beginning to understand Arthur Miller's contribution to American theater, art, and consciousness. This recognition of his long and prolific career climaxed when Miller won the Kennedy Center Honors Award for distinguished lifetime achievement in 1984. At the award banquet a powerful irony struck the playwright; the ceremony was held in the same room in which Miller faced the House Un-American Activities Committee almost thirty years earlier.

CONCLUSION

Miller's most recent plays have not enjoyed successful theatrical runs. In 1991 his play *The Ride Down Mt. Morgan* premiered in London, but ran for only three months. His latest play, *The Last Yankee*, a comedy-drama, also suffered a short life span after it opened in 1993 at the Manhattan Theatre Club in New York. Now in his eighties, Miller is still working.

In his autobiography, it is apparent that the experiences of Miller's life have merged with his artistic goals to create a very personal body of work. The impact of his family, the depression, his discovery of drama at the University of Michigan, his unfortunate standoff with HUAC, his marriages, his political activism as president of PEN, his protest of the war in Vietnam, and his ongoing relationship with the theater, its critics, and its audiences have all coalesced to shape the form and power of his plays.

The characters in Miller's dramas act out human concerns that engage the playwright personally. He calls on his characters to take responsibility for their actions, and Miller himself never shies away from his responsibility to act on his own convictions. Miller rejects self-pity in his characters, and he consistently rebounds from harsh criticism. Miller wants his characters to find the strength to overcome moral paralysis and act on the world, and Miller sticks to his moral beliefs against popular opinion. In a sense Miller is similar to Ben in *Death of a Salesman*—he went into the "jungle" and came out a success; he did not succumb to the nullifying illusions that defeated Willy Loman. He carried on a dialogue with himself, his family, and his audience that continues to this day. Miller lives with his wife Inge at the same home in Roxbury, Connecticut, that he purchased after the success of *All My Sons.* He is a grandfather to his son's three children; his two daughters, Rebecca and Jane, are both involved in the arts; and his wife's love of photography continues.

Throughout his career, Miller's works reveal the idea that beneath the chaos of reality there are hidden forces that connect all human beings to one another and to the world. It is with this major theme that Miller chooses to end his autobiography. Pondering the coyotes that he can see outside his Roxbury studio window, Miller writes, "I am a mystery to them until they tire of it and move on, but the truth, the first truth, probably, is that we are all connected, watching one another." As thousands of audiences watch the interior workings of Arthur Miller unfold on stage, the playwright moves them to wonder about that truth.

CHAPTER 1

Themes

The Thematic Structure in *Death of a Salesman*

Edward Murray

Edward Murray praises Miller for integrating individual character struggles with larger social complexities in *Death of a Salesman*. In the play, the characters must struggle with the drive for personal freedom and the forces of society that work to deny it. According to Murray, Miller has created a complex vision of human experience in *Death of a Salesman*. The playwright does not offer one profound universal solution to understand the modern experience, rather he poses questions: How does one know what is right to do? and How does one reconcile human values in a dehumanizing economic society?

Edward Murray is a professor of English at State University of New York College at Brockport. His works include *Clifford Odets: The Thirties and After*, *Ten Film Classics*, and *The Cinematic Imagination: Writers and the Motion Pictures*. Murray is a contributor to *College Language Association Journal* and *Literature/Film Quarterly*.

Critics of *Death of a Salesman*, when they have not been vexed by the problem of genre—a problem that will be taken up at the end of this viewpoint—have most often been concerned with two aspects of the theme: 1) unity of conception; and 2) the values inherent in Miller's "counterweight" to Willy Loman's "wrong dreams."

Is the "system" to blame for Willy's fate, ask some critics, or is the fault within Willy's character? Is there a "split" here between "personal" (or "Freudian") and "social" (or "Marxian") motivation? Moreover, Miller's "positive" values, some critics urge, reveal a "romantic" and "sentimental" view of man—that is, Biff's emphasis on "freedom and the body," "self-realization," and "the simple life" are "romantic" and "sentimental"—while the references to Willy's working with his hands is an inadequate solution to the problems posed by the play. Few Americans, it has also been alleged, believe with Willy Loman that success depends on being "well liked."

THEMATIC UNITY IN *DEATH OF A SALESMAN*

Criticism of thematic unity in *Salesman,* it is obvious, betrays a curious "either-or" kind of thinking. Usually Miller is pummeled for too overtly trying to "prove the theme," but with *Salesman* the strategy has been to attack him for being too "realistic." Actually Miller should be praised for having succeeded in the difficult task of integrating the "personal" and the "social" in his play. Notice, for example, that Biff more than once calls Willy a "fake." Although this word has a double reference in the play, thematically it is all of a piece. Willy is a "fake" for being unfaithful to Linda; he is also a "fake" as a salesman, for he is nothing but an unsuccessful "drummer." Moreover, Willy's values are "fake," since they stem from his "phony dream." Nor is Willy's infidelity merely "personal"—it results from his loneliness (loneliness which has a "social" dimension, since it is a necessary concomitant of his work role) and his anxiety to keep ahead of other salesmen in a competitive society. The hotel scene is central because it crystallizes for Biff, Willy's essential falseness; that is, it leads to Biff's questioning of *all* Willy's values, and his eventual rejection of them. True, Biff would probably have "failed" (however defined) in business anyway; but the hotel scene is also linked to the play's climax, for Biff's insight into Willy and his "spiteful" attitude toward him is a preparation for his insight into himself and his subsequent acceptance of himself. To ask a modern dramatist to write a play that emphasizes *either* social necessity *or* individual responsibility would seem to involve an oversimplified approach to experience. The abstract discussion of freedom versus determinism, usually conducted in a philosophical vacuum, seems ultimately a dead end; in actuality, we recognize the rival claims of both factors, and we manage to live with both. As in *All My Sons*, Miller appears to affirm freedom at the same time that he underlines the influence of social forces. A Charley can remain fundamentally decent in spite of the negative elements in society. A

Ben (at least Willy's version of Ben) can succeed ruthlessly, but remain self-assured and apparently free from guilt. The same might be said of Howard. Willy, on the other hand, loses his way in such a world—and who can determine the exact degree of his culpability? (In Nazi Germany, although some men lost their integrity, some men did not; but it does not follow that there were no evil forces in German society.) How separate the "social" from the "personal" in *Salesman*? Willy, for example, has deep-rooted feelings of insecurity: "Dad left when I was such a baby and . . . I still feel—kind of temporary about myself." This sounds "personal." But would Willy have felt so "temporary" in a society that offered more community, more "comradeship"? Surely it is trite to observe that a society such as ours, with shifting social values, hardly furnishes an ideal structure for self-discovery. *Death of a Salesman* reflects the density and complexity of life itself. Why then must we choose either "personal" or "social," either "political" or "sexual" explanations? Why "Freudianism" or "Marxism"? "Freudianism" and "Marxism" are, like *Salesman*, abstractions from life; but if "Freudianism" and "Marxism" are "total ideologies" and "mutually exclusive," that does not mean that *Salesman* cannot use both "ideologies," for a play does not project "total ideologies" (except thesis plays), but assimilates "totalities" to its own unique pattern and design.

WILLY'S MISGUIDED DREAMS

In the Requiem, Miller seems quite explicit about what "wrong dreams" possessed Willy; Happy says: "[Willy] had a good dream. It's the only dream you can have—to come out number-one man." Why must Charley necessarily speak for Miller? (Are we always sure who speaks for Shakespeare?) It is not true that the scene as a whole speaks of *the* salesman; only Charley speaks of *the* salesman—the other characters speak of Willy. And the answer to, Who was Willy? is suggested in Biff's remark that "There's more of [Willy] in that front stoop than in all the sales he ever made"; it is implied in Happy's statement (above), for Willy was less than the "number-one man"; and Willy, like Biff (Miller seems to imply), should have accepted his limitations. Biff's objection to Willy appears to be that Willy defines himself too narrowly in terms of his social role. Is Charley's definition of Willy in respect to *the* salesman confusing? Is Charley out of character here? Miller says: "In all [Charley] says, despite what he says, there is pity. . . ." In the action of the play, Charley speaks hard: "When a deposit bottle is broken you don't get your nickel back"; "My salvation is that I never took any interest in anything"; "The only thing you got in this world is what you can sell." Yet Charley comes in the middle of the night to cheer Willy; he "lends" Willy fifty dollars a week; and he endures Willy's insults for years. This shows that Charley is not so hard as he pretends, that we need not take at face value all that he says. Aside from this, there seems to be no necessary inconsistency in Charley's Requiem speech. Previously, Charley has said that—in the broad sense—we are all salesmen; what he has debunked throughout the play is Willy's belief in "personality" ("Who liked J.P. Morgan?" asks Charley). In his farewell to Willy, however, perhaps out of his characteristic pity, he seems to be softening his previous debunking, he seems to be saying that so long as there *are* salesmen—in the narrow sense now—then *that* kind of "salesman is got to dream. . . . It comes with the territory." Charley would seem, then, to be merely "realistic." Moreover, perhaps a part of Charley's function in the Requiem is to speak only good of the dead, in an effort to hearten Willy's widow. If this reading is valid, Charley remains in character.

It is difficult, however, to justify Linda's final speech: "Why did you do it? I search and search and I search, and I can't understand it, Willy." True, even an expected event might cause surprise—rational understanding cannot prevent emotional shock, especially in the case of a loved one's suicide. Linda, moreover, being sympathetic but not very perceptive, could never enter wholly into Willy's dreams— she was different in that she could "walk away" ("life is a casting off," she says). Nevertheless, one feels that there is a spurious element here—an abandonment of logic for the sake of a "curtain." Linda knew of Willy's previous suicide attempts; she knew of his depression over Biff and the job; and she knew a great deal about Willy's dreams. There would seem to be very little, really, to search for on Linda's part. The one thing that Linda knew nothing about was Willy's infidelity; but Willy's infidelity was not causally related to his suicide. In spite of the fact that much of the specific content of the Requiem is defensible, however, it still seems unsatisfactory. Technically, as has been said, it violates the convention of point of view, and, although it helps to focus the theme, it says nothing really new, nothing that has not been better expressed in the previous action. Moreover, in its final utterance, it is even somewhat specious and confusing.

MILLER'S VISION OF EXPERIENCE

With such terms in mind as "freedom and the body," "self-realization," and "the simple life," a reading of Plato's *Republic* might suggest that the Greeks, far from being "classical," were in reality extremely "romantic." The "classical-romantic" dichotomy thus becomes semantically meaningless. Equally unsatisfactory are vague terms like "nature" and "individualism." The critical question is whether Miller has rendered a complex vision of experience, not whether the critic necessarily agrees with the alleged interpretation of the vision. The play implies that Willy might have been happier in a pre- "capitalistic" (or perhaps pre-industrial) society; it more plainly suggests that Willy would have been happier working with his "hands"; and it makes manifest that Biff feels that—*for him*—the West is the answer. Psychologically, it is a truism to say that a man will be happy doing what he can do best. What appears to disturb some critics is that this "answer" is not "profound" enough. Would Oedipus[1] have brought on his fate if he had not been rash? Would Lear[2] have ended badly had he not been short-tempered? How "profound" are the specific "counter-weights" here? Moreover, is Miller offering a "universal" solution to a modern problem? Obviously not; not all men are good with their "hands" (Charley, for example); and it is precisely the point that Biff's "solution" is unique—doesn't he say: "I know who I am"? Biff speaks for Biff. Furthermore, *Salesman* raises questions that can never be answered in a scientific way. Was it really "better" in pre-"capitalistic" America? Historically, of course, the economic and social transformation of American society had already begun when, in terms of the play, Willy's father sold flutes across the country. *In terms of the play,* however, there is no "proof" that Miller is "saying" that pre-"capitalistic" society was "better"—for the contrast between "past" and "present" is limited by point of view, and the "past" is wholly Willy's projection. As for the positive values that seem to emerge from the play—"romantic" and "sentimental" values—one might fairly ask whether they are quite

---

1. tragic hero in *Oedipus Rex* by Sophocles 2. tragic hero in Shakespeare's *King Lear*

so shoddy as some critics would have us believe. These same critics would have to hold (and perhaps some do) that the democratic experiment is shoddy, that it is "romantic" and "sentimental," since these same values are part of the democratic rhetoric. Not all of us, however, have lost faith in that rhetoric. *Salesman* also poses questions which, it is hoped, are answerable, but which as yet have not been answered— such as, how are we to reconcile human values with an expanding economy of abundance which puts a premium on mechanization and impersonality? Critics who assault *Salesman* rarely reveal where *they* stand; they seem to suggest that the answer has been found—perhaps they themselves have the answer—but that Miller, through sheer stupidity or perversity, has not provided the answer. Some critics miss the theological and metaphysical dimension in *Salesman*; but in a pluralistic society such as ours it is surely arrogant to demand a single standard.

The Author Reflects on *Death of a Salesman*

Arthur Miller

Arthur Miller writes that the first vague idea he had of *Death of a Salesman* was an image of an enormous face that filled the height of a stage proscenium arch. In this excerpt, the playwright explains that he wanted to move inside this head of Willy Loman and express the salesman's way of thinking. Just as thoughts jump across the mind, he envisioned the form of the play jumping back-and-forth from present and past and from events to consequences.

Miller is surprised at the numerous and various interpretations that the play has spawned. Miller maintains that he intended the play to portray simple images of things like home, aging, family relation-ships, and, most importantly, the desire for an individual to leave a "thumbprint" on the world. Miller argues that he wanted to pierce through the usual theatrical conventions to get to the heart of a scene, to eliminate dramatic transitions, and find an economy of motion, moments, and words.

The first image that occurred to me which was to result in *Death of a Salesman* was of an enormous face the height of the proscenium arch which would appear and then open up, and we would see the inside of a man's head. In fact, *The Inside of His Head* was the first title. It was conceived half in laughter, for the inside of his head was a mass of contradictions. The image was in direct opposition to the method of *All My Sons*—a method one might call linear or eventual in that one fact or incident creates the necessity for the next. The *Salesman* image was from the beginning absorbed with the concept that nothing in life comes "next" but that everything exists together and at the same time within us; that there is no past to be "brought

Reprinted from the Introduction to *Arthur Miller's Collected Plays*, by Arthur Miller. Copyright © 1957 by Arthur Miller. Used by permission of Viking Penguin, a division of Penguin Putnam Inc.

forward" in a human being, but that he is his past at every moment and that the present is merely that which his past is capable of noticing and smelling and reacting to.

THE PLAY'S DRAMATIC FORM

I wished to create a form which, in itself as a form, would literally be the process of Willy Loman's way of mind. But to say "wished" is not accurate. Any dramatic form is an artifice, a way of transforming a subjective feeling into something that can be comprehended through public symbols. Its efficiency as a form is to be judged—at least by the writer—by how much of the original vision and feeling is lost or distorted by this transformation. I wished to speak of the salesman most precisely as I felt about him, to give no part of that feeling away for the sake of any effect or any dramatic necessity. What was wanted now was not a mounting line of tension, nor a gradually narrowing cone of intensifying suspense, but a bloc, a single chord presented as such at the outset, within which all the strains and melodies would already be contained. The strategy, as with *All My Sons,* was to appear entirely unstrategic but with a difference. This time, if I could, I would have told the whole story and set forth all the characters in one unbroken speech or even one sentence or a single flash of light. As I look at the play now its form seems the form of a confession, for that is how it is told, now speaking of what happened yesterday, then suddenly following some connection to a time twenty years ago, then leaping even further back and then returning to the present and even speculating about the future.

Where in *All My Sons* it had seemed necessary to prove the connections between the present and the past, between events and moral consequences, between the manifest and the hidden, in this play all was assumed as proven to begin with. All I was doing was bringing things to mind. The assumption, also, was that everyone knew Willy Loman. I can realize this only now, it is true, but it is equally apparent to me that I took it somehow for granted then. There was still the attitude of the unveiler, but no bringing together of hitherto unrelated things; only pre-existing images, events, confrontations, moods, and pieces of knowledge. So there was a kind of confidence underlying this play which the form itself expresses, even a naïveté, a self-disarming quality that was in part born of my belief in the audience as being essentially the same as myself. If I had wanted, then, to put the audience reaction into words, it would not have been "What happens next and why?" so much as "Oh, God, of course!". . .

INTERPRETATIONS OF THE PLAY

A great deal has been said and written about what *Death of a Salesman* is supposed to signify, both psychologically and from the socio-political viewpoints. For instance, in one periodical of the far Right it was called a "time bomb expertly placed under the edifice of Americanism," while the *Daily Worker* reviewer thought it entirely decadent. In Catholic Spain it ran longer than any modern play and it has been refused production in Russia but not, from time to time, in certain satellite countries, depending on the direction and velocity of the wind. The Spanish press, thoroughly controlled by Catholic orthodoxy, regarded the play as commendable proof of the spirit's death where there is no God. In America, even as it was being cannonaded as a piece of Communist propaganda, two of the largest manufacturing corporations in the country invited me to address their sales organizations in conventions assembled, while the road company was here and there picketed by the Catholic War Veterans and the American Legion. It made only a fair impression in London, but in the area of the Norwegian Arctic Circle fishermen whose only contact with civilization was the radio and the occasional visit of the government boat insisted on seeing it night after night—the same few people—believing it to be some kind of religious rite. One organization of salesmen raised me up nearly to patron-sainthood, and another, a national sales managers' group, complained that the difficulty of recruiting salesmen was directly traceable to the play. When the movie was made, the producing company got so frightened it produced a sort of trailer to be shown before the picture, a documentary short film which demonstrated how exceptional Willy Loman was; how necessary selling is to the economy; how secure the salesman's life really is; how idiotic, in short, was the feature film they had just spent more than a million dollars to produce. Fright does odd things to people.

On the psychological front the play spawned a small hill of doctoral theses explaining its Freudian symbolism, and there were innumerable letters asking if I was aware that the fountain pen which Biff steals is a phallic symbol. Some, on the other hand, felt it was merely a fountain pen and dismissed the whole play. I received visits from men over sixty from as far away as California who had come across the country to have me write the stories of their lives, because the story of Willy Loman was exactly like theirs. The letters from women made it clear that the central character of the play was Linda; sons saw the entire action revolving around Biff or Happy, and fathers wanted advice, in effect, on how to avoid parricide. Probably the most succinct reaction to the play was voiced by a man who, on leaving the theater, said, "I always said that New England territory was no damned good." This, at least, was a fact.

That I have and had not the slightest interest in the selling profession is probably unbelievable to most people, and I very early gave up trying even to say so. And when asked what Willy was selling, what was in his bags, I could only reply, "Himself." I was trying neither to condemn a profession nor particularly to improve it, and, I will admit, I was little better than ignorant of Freud's teachings when I wrote it. There was no attempt to bring down the American edifice nor to raise it higher, to show up family relations or to cure the ills afflicting that inevitable institution. The truth, at least of my aim—which is all I can speak of authoritatively—is much simpler and more complex.

THE PLAY'S ESSENTIAL IMAGES

The play grew from simply images. From a little frame house on a street of little frame houses, which had once been loud with the noise of growing boys, and then was empty and silent and finally occupied by strangers. Strangers who could not know with what conquistadorial joy Willy and his boys had once re-shingled the roof. Now it was quiet in the house, and the wrong people in the beds.

It grew from images of futility—the cavernous Sunday afternoons polishing the car. Where is that car now? And the chamois cloths carefully washed and put up to dry, where are the chamois cloths?

And the endless, convoluted discussions, wonderments, arguments, belittlements, encouragements, fiery resolutions, abdications, returns, partings, voyages out and voyages back, tremendous opportunities and small, squeaking denouements—and all in the kitchen now occupied by strangers who cannot hear what the walls are saying.

The image of aging and so many of your friends already gone and strangers in the seats of the mighty who do not know you or your triumphs or your incredible value.

The image of the son's hard, public eye upon you, no longer swept by your myth, no longer rousable from his separateness, no longer knowing you have lived for him and have wept for him.

The image of ferocity when love has turned to something else and yet is there, is somewhere in the room if one could only find it.

The image of people turning into strangers who only evaluate one another.

Above all, perhaps, the image of a need greater than hunger or sex or thirst, a need to leave a thumbprint somewhere on the world. A need for immortality, and by admitting it, the knowing that one has carefully inscribed one's name on a cake of ice on a hot July day.

I sought the relatedness of all things by isolating their unrelatedness, a man superbly alone with his sense of not having touched, and finally knowing in his last extremity that the love which had always been in the room unlocated was now found.

The image of a suicide so mixed in motive as to be unfathomable and yet demanding statement. Revenge was in it and a power of love, a victory in that it would bequeath a fortune to the living and a flight from emptiness. With it an image of peace at the final curtain, the peace that is between wars, the peace leaving the issues above ground and viable yet.

And always, throughout, the image of private man in a world full of strangers, a world that is not home nor even an open battleground but only galaxies of high promise over a fear of falling.

And the image of a man making something with his hands being a rock to touch and return to. "He was always so wonderful with his hands," says his wife over his grave, and I laughed when the line came, laughed with the artist-devil's laugh, for it had all come together in this line, she having been made by him though he did not know it or believe in it or receive it into himself. Only rank, height of power, the sense of having won he believed was real—the galaxy thrust up into the sky by projectors on the rooftops of the city he believed were real stars.

THE PLAY'S STRUCTURAL ORGANIZATION

It came from structural images. The play's eye was to revolve from within Willy's head, sweeping endlessly in all directions like a light on the sea, and nothing that formed in the distant mist was to be left uninvestigated. It was thought of as having the density of the novel form in its interchange of viewpoints, so that while all roads led to Willy the other characters were to feel it was their play, a story about them and not him.

There were two undulating lines in mind, one above the other, the past webbed to the present moving on together in him and sometimes openly joined and once, finally, colliding in the showdown which defined him in his eyes at least—and so to sleep.

Above all, in the structural sense, I aimed to make a play with the veritable countenance of life. To make one the many, as in life, so that "society" is a power and a mystery of custom and inside the man and surrounding him, as the fish is in the sea and the sea inside the fish, his birthplace and burial ground, promise and threat. To speak commonsensically of social facts which every businessman knows and talks about but which are too prosaic to mention or are usually fancied up on the stage as philosophical problems. When a man gets old you fire him, you have to, he can't do the work. To speak and even to celebrate the common sense of businessmen, who love the personality that wins the day but know that you've got to have the right goods at the right price, handsome and well-spoken as you are. (To some, these were scandalous and infamous arraignments of society when uttered in the context of art. But not to the businessmen themselves; they knew it was all true and I cherished their clear-eyed talk.)

The image of a play without transitional scenes was there in the beginning. There was too much to say to waste precious stage time with feints and preparations, in themselves agonizing "structural" bridges for a writer to work out since they are not why he is writing. There was a resolution, as in *All My Sons*, not to waste motion or moments, but in this case to shear through everything up to the meat of a scene; a resolution not to write an unmeant word for the sake of the form but to make the form give and stretch and contract for the sake of the thing to be said. To cling to the process of Willy's mind as the form the story would take.

The Ethic of Success in *Death of a Salesman*

Robert N. Wilson

In order to understand the social pressure to achieve presented in *Death of a Salesman*, Robert N. Wilson outlines sociologist Robert K. Merton's model for coping with the American success ethic. Wilson argues that each character uses a strategy or combination of strategies from Merton's model. Willy, for example, stubbornly employs conformity to fulfill society's expectations for success, even when it is futile. Wilson suggests that Ben, Willy's brother, represents Merton's strategy of innovation, achieving his goal of success outside the approved societal means. Willy's sons, Biff and Happy, have been coached by their father to use the style of conformity where personality and popularity take precedence over industriousness. Ultimately, according to Wilson, Biff uses Merton's strategy of retreatism by essentially dropping out of society entirely. Happy, however, remains entrenched in the same kind of empty conformity that destroys his father.

Robert N. Wilson is a professor of sociology at the University of North Carolina at Chapel Hill. In addition to *The Writer as Seer*, he has written *Man Made Plain: The Poet in Contemporary Society* and *The Arts in Society*.

We need to look more closely into the nature of success and into its social context in the United States. In this effort we can begin with a model first advanced by Robert K. Merton in his germinal essay "Social Structure and Anomie." Merton distinguishes two major features of the social structure—cultural goals and institutional norms. Cultural goals consist of the ends toward which we strive, in Willy Loman's case the image of the master salesman, esteemed by all and almost effortlessly able to move his goods and earn a comfortable living. . . .

Willy's goal, then, reiterated in many guises throughout the course of the play, is to achieve as a salesman; but perhaps more important, it is to be "remembered and loved and helped by so many different people.". . .

Our culture has consistently exhorted the individual to strive for transcendent success. Today's inciting language is probably less vulgar (and also less honest) than the strident nineteenth-century pronouncements of an Andrew Carnegie—"Say each to yourself: 'My place is at the top.' Be king in your dreams"—or a Russell H. Conwell—"I say that you ought to get rich, and it is your duty to get rich"; "The idea is that in this country of ours every man has the opportunity to make more of himself than he does in his own environment, with his own skill, with his own energy, and with his own friends." But one may doubt that the substance of the message has changed much. The transition from Andrew Carnegie to Dale Carnegie, epitomized by David Riesman as "from the invisible hand to the glad hand," entails less emphasis on capital formation and more on the charms of leadership style, but the aim is still to be a winner in a very competitive game, whose rules are as vague as its scoreboard is explicit. In Merton's axiom of striving, one should regard the situation as fluid, never foreclosing one's chances, and should identify oneself with those at the top whom one will sooner or later join. And we are enjoined, further, to think that energetic ambition is in some sense a moral obligation, a responsibility devolving solely on the individual, to be honored even in the situation of patent failure.

ROBERT MERTON'S STRATEGIES FOR SUCCESS

Willy Loman is an exemplar of just these values. In fact, each of the figures in *Death of a Salesman* may be viewed as enmeshed in this set of circumstances, and each takes some path of action in the effort to deal with them. Merton sets forth a number of alternate strategies an individual might adopt in trying to cope with the American success ethic. He arranges them in a seemingly simple but remarkably stimulating model:

Conformity—accepting both conventional cultural goals and approved institutional means of reaching them

Innovation—accepting the goals but rejecting the fully legitimate means

Ritualism—rejecting or withdrawing from the goals, but dutifully adhering to the means

Retreatism—shunning both the goals and the means; essentially, not playing the game

Rebellion—substituting new values in the realms of both goals and means

Obviously, very few people could be expected to cling uniformly to a single one of these strategies throughout life; almost all actual behavior is composed of mixed strategies, and people shift their emphases in tune with life's exigencies. Nevertheless, it is fair to say that each of Miller's characters seizes one of these patterns as his dominant mode for coming to grips with the imperatives of success. . . .

WILLY'S CONFORMITY

Willy Loman's path is primarily that of conformity. Indeed, one of the saddest aspects of his story lies in his stubborn, futile effort to do what is expected of him; then, having played by the rules as he conceives them and having held a bright image of achievement in mind, he is unfairly deprived of his just reward. Thus Willy laments, in dialogue with his wife:

WILLY: Figure it out. Work a lifetime to pay off a house. You finally own it, and there's nobody to live in it.

LINDA: Well, dear, life is a casting off. It's always that way.

WILLY: No, no, some people—some people accomplish something.

Especially in his earlier years, Willy embraces the dominant values of his culture and struggles to reach them through legitimate techniques. He has never really been very successful, but he has admired those who made it and he has held out hope. His sense of the imperative is so overpowering that he is forced to lie to himself and his sons, to buck himself up with a threnody of exhortation and might have been. He doggedly believes in his society as the land of opportunity. But Willy does not realize that "personality" and friendship are not enough. In the contemporary United States occupational conduct is more clearly governed by "universalism (not who you are, but what you can do) and "functional specificity" (not the valuing of the total man, but of his specific skills and contributions to some enterprise). So Willy's best friend Charley tries to enlighten him:

WILLY: Charley, I'm strapped. I'm strapped. I don't know what to do. I was just fired.

CHARLEY: Howard fired you?

WILLY: That snotnose. Imagine that? I named him. I named him Howard.

CHARLEY: Willy, when're you gonna realize that them things don't mean anything? You named him Howard, but you can't sell that. The only thing you got in this world is what you can sell. And the funny thing is that you're a salesman, and you don't know that.

WILLY: I've always tried to think otherwise, I guess. I always felt that if a man was impressive, and well liked, that nothing—

CHARLEY: Why must everybody like you? Who liked J.P. Morgan? Was he impressive? In a Turkish bath he'd look like a butcher. But with his pockets on he was very well liked.

Willy, however, cannot bring himself to understand. He talks of his n'er-do-well older son, Biff: "Biff Loman is lost. In the greatest country in the world a young man with such personal attractiveness, gets lost."

As life closes in on him in the form of time payments, disappointing children, failing energies, and the bald truth that the Dave Singleman legend is not to be his, Willy slips more nearly into *ritualism.* He still plays the game and abides by the rules but doesn't truly hope for economic success; he emphasizes his manual talents more strongly and his wish to raise chickens at a little place in the country. Finally he follows an unusual form of innovation: desperately wanting the success goals for his sons, he uses illegitimate means to provide them with money—that is, the proceeds of his life insurance policy, the only tangible thing he has to give them. From another perspective, Willy's suicide could be seen as the ultimate in *retreatism,* the final turning away from a life and a society that have perhaps failed him as much as he has failed them. Suicide, given Willy's hopes for his boys and his dutifulness toward his wife, may be for him the closest approximation of the more common kinds of retreatism such as Skid Row.

THE SUCCESS OF CHARLEY AND BERNARD

Willy's friend and neighbor, Charley, exemplifies *conformity,* accepting both the goal of success and the approved routes to its attainment. He and his son, Bernard, form a counterpoint to Willy and his boys; Charley and Bernard are realists, appraising their circumstance with clear eye and hard head. Their facility in "making it" is presented to us in recurrent contrast to the windy, aimless thrashing about of the Lomans, impaled between dreams and incompetence. We are offered few details of Charley's successful coping. He appears as a shrewd if largely unheeded counselor to Willy, and as a businessman comfortable enough to subsidize Willy's declining months. Bernard's career, traced in somewhat more detail, is the classic American success story of our era. Thematically, it is sharply opposed to the drifting noncareers of Biff and Happy Loman. At least two facets of Bernard's history are especially significant in the light of contemporary social structure. The first is the value he places on education, which is, as we know, more and more often *the* path to occupational achievement. Bernard learns his lessons well; he is groomed by the school system and his parents to value both academic attainment per se and the complex of motivations surrounding it. A "good boy" conforming to all expectations, he reaps a good boy's rewards. The second striking element in Bernard is the symbolic import of his career, the meaning of appearing as a lawyer before the Supreme Court. Here Miller has chosen both a high-prestige profession—in some ways today the case type of conforming careerism—and an institution, the Supreme Court, that stands at the very peak of American occupational esteem. Finally, the scene between Bernard and Willy in Charley's office and the ensuing conversation Willy has with Charley underline again the distinctions between a fulfilling and an unfulfilling conformity. We have once more the contrast of charm versus competence, seeming versus doing.

> WILLY: The Supreme Court! And he didn't even mention it!
>
> CHARLEY: He don't have to—he's gonna do it.

BEN'S SUCCESS STRATEGY

Willy's brother, Ben, represents *innovation* in Merton's analysis. He has fully adopted the goal of material success but has apparently taken unusual and not entirely approved means to realize the goal. He has gone outside the framework of his society as an adventurer in the Alaska of that day, presumably the twenties and thirties. His business ethics are questionable, as indicated in the scene in which he trips Biff with his cane and comments, "Never fight fair with a stranger, boy. You'll never get out of the jungle that way." Like many innovators—the Robber Barons of the late nineteenth century, the gangsters of the twentieth—Ben has a glamorous aura. People like Ben have often been admired in American life, especially by the conforming or ritualistic

Willys, who see in the Bens a confirmation of the cultural promise. Thus Willy describes Ben's success: "What's the mystery? The man knew what he wanted and went out and got it! Walked into a jungle, and comes out, the age of twenty-one, and he's rich!"

It is true, as Schneider[1] observes, that the heart of *Death of a Salesman* is the complex relationships between Willy and his sons and between the two sets of brothers (Willy and Ben, Biff and Happy). The dynamics of this interplay, punctuated by affection, jealousy, high expectations and cruel recriminations, are the threads that lead us through Willy's disaster. But the primary sociological point is these relationships all find their focus, their emotional field of force, in the occupational world and the success ethic. We have seen how Willy and Ben take different paths and how Ben represents for Willy a brutal, flashy alternative to the success image of Dave Singleman. How do Biff and Happy respond to the challenges inherent in Merton's model of ends and means?

THE FAILURE OF THE LOMAN BROTHERS

The Loman brothers grow up nourished by their father's misguided but potent success dream. Throughout their lives Willy devotes himself to coaching them, almost like an older teammate, in the techniques for winning the striving game. He stresses, of course, those tactics he believes to be the keys to achievement: popularity, congeniality, physical prowess, attractiveness—in a phrase, the cult of personality. Willy never tells the boys they need skill or industriousness; indeed, he sedulously encourages them, especially Biff, in cutting corners and relying on personal magnetism to carry the day. One might say he determinedly sells them the bill of goods he has once been sold, infecting the next generation with the vocational pathology whose symptoms bring him down.

Biff, the older son, appears to fit the pattern of *retreatism*. We feel occasionally that if Biff had more energy and stability of purpose he might pursue *rebellion*; yet his rebellion only flickers in the desert of his nomadic drifting, as in his dream of an outdoor life far from the rat race. Although Biff pays sporadic lip service to the cultural goals, partly in a futile effort to buck up the sagging Willy, he really has withdrawn his allegiance from both common goals and common

1. American psychiatrist and author

means. His wandering in the West is an escape from the competitive occupational world, just as it is an escape from the father whose infidelity makes him feel sexually betrayed. He vaguely yearns for something different but does not have the qualities to articulate and search out that "something." Biff's attitudes and behavior add up to a bitter caricature of a man, trapped by the success ethic, floundering as his father flounders: "I tell ya, Hap, I don't know what the future is. I don't know—what I'm supposed to want. . . . And always to have to get ahead of the next fella. And still—that's how you build a future. . . . I've always made a point of not wasting my life, and everytime I come back here I know that all I've done is to waste my life."

Happy seems harder to place in Merton's terms but is generally *conforming*. Although his sharp business practices may incline toward *innovation* on the style of his Uncle Ben, his is a kind of empty conformity. Happy gets, in modest measure, what he thinks he wants, but his life is somehow flavorless, without bite or savor. He is the one character many critics of the play have found puzzling and inconsistent with the master themes of the drama. Schneider goes so far as to suggest that the play might be seen as a dream of Happy, that he stands outside the main flow of action.

Linda, wife and mother, is obviously the linchpin that holds the Loman family together, as nearly as they may be said to cohere. Of course, in her role she does not confront the occupational strife as a direct participant; nevertheless, the strains of all three male Lomans lap over into her life. Hers is the voice of sweet reason, of the wise, resigned observer. But with all her understanding of what makes Willy run, she is powerless to stop the onrush of failure and doom. Linda's chosen path is *ritualism*. She keeps on keeping on but asks wearily, "Why must everybody conquer the world?"

Marxism and *Death of a Salesman*

Dennis Welland

Dennis Welland rejects the literary interpretations of
critics Eric Bentley and Eleanor Clark that link *Death
of a Salesman* to Marxist and socialist theory. Welland
argues that the critical office scene where Willy loses
his job does not portray Howard, the boss, as a ruthless executive destroying the lowly common man; instead, Willy is more a victim of his own past than he
is of capitalism. Although one can sympathize with
Willy's dilemma, one cannot respect the bungling
salesman. Ironically, Charley is more of a successful
capitalist than Howard, and it is Charley who not only
understands Willy's plight but also gives him money
and offers him a job. According to Welland, Miller
does not indict big business and he does not present a
noticeably Marxist position.

Dennis Welland is a professor of American litera-
ture at Victoria University in Manchester, England.
His works include *Mark Twain in England, The
United States: A Companion to American Studies,*
and *Benjamin Franklin: Autobiography and Other
Pieces.*

Discussion of *Death of a Salesman* has always been bedev-
illed by the question: is it a tragedy? The success of its New
York presentation—its 742 performances put it among the
fifty longest recorded Broadway runs, and it took both the
Drama Critics' and the Pulitzer prizes—did not prevent, indeed perhaps invited, hostility. Eric Bentley, abroad when it
opened in February 1949, attacked it on his return and hit
hard at everything from the lighting to the language, directing his onslaught particularly at what he saw as the play's
conflicting aims:

Reprinted from *Arthur Miller,* by Dennis Welland (New York: Grove Press). Copyright
© 1961 by Dennis Welland. Used by permission of the author.

CRITICISM OF *DEATH OF A SALESMAN*

> The "tragedy" destroys the social drama; the social drama keeps the "tragedy" from having a genuinely tragic stature. By this last remark I mean that the theme of this social drama, as of most others, is *the little man as victim.* The theme arouses pity but no terror. Man is here too little and too passive to play the tragic hero.

> More important even than this, the tragedy and the social drama actually conflict. The tragic catharsis reconciles us to, or persuades us to disregard, precisely those material conditions which the social drama calls our attention to. . . . Or is Mr. Miller a "tragic" artist who without knowing it has been confused by Marxism?

Exactly the reverse hypothesis was advanced by Eleanor Clark in *Partisan Review*; she saw Miller as a Marxist who had been confused by tragedy:

> It is, of course, the capitalist system that has done Willy in; the scene in which he is brutally fired after some forty years with the firm comes straight from the party-line literature of the 'thirties, and the idea emerges lucidly enough through all the confused motivations of the play that it is our particular form of money economy that has bred the absurdly false ideals of both father and sons. It emerges, however, like a succession of shots from a duck-blind. Immediately after every crack the playwright withdraws behind an air of pseudo-universality, and hurries to present some cruelty or misfortune due either to Willy's own weakness, as when he refuses his friend's offer of a job after he has been fired, or gratuitously from some other source, as in the quite unbelievable scene of the two sons walking out on their father in the restaurant.

The whole play, for Miss Clark, is characterised by

> an intellectual muddle and a lack of candor that regardless of Mr. Miller's conscious intent are the main earmark of contemporary fellow-traveling. What used to be a roar has become a whine.

At about the time of the play's opening, Miller himself, interviewed by the *New York Times*, stressed the tragic intention:

> The tragic feeling is evoked in us when we are in the presence of a character who is ready to lay down his life, if need be, to secure one thing—his sense of personal dignity.

Important as this idea is in Miller's later plays, it was confusing when associated with *Death of a Salesman*, for critics were quick to point out what the play itself demonstrated— that Willy Loman's sense of personal dignity was too precariously based to give him heroic stature. Since then it has become tediously conventional for the writers of books surveying modern drama to praise the play's social realism but hurriedly to add that, of course, it falls short of tragedy and is therefore disqualified as a "great play." (This complaint is usually associated with strictures on its unpoetic use of language.)

What is irritating about such criticism is its assured conviction that the mixture of social drama and tragedy is unintentional, and its implication that, if Miller had only been clear-minded enough to concentrate on one or the other, a better play would have resulted. Better or not, it would have been a totally different play, and for once the audiences who took the play that was offered to them seem wiser than *genre*-minded critics who wanted something else. Eric Bentley is perfectly right to see it as a play about "the little man as victim," but less right when he seems to prefer the little man to be a victim of only one thing, and to assume that a "social drama" must be a socialist drama. The Marxist plays of Clifford Odets in the nineteen-thirties had rarely communicated a sense of the complex density of the society they criticised, and merely to show the little man as the victim of capitalist big business would, in 1949, have been "picayune," to use one of Miller's own words: Elmer Rice had done that well enough in *The Adding Machine* twenty-six years earlier.

MARXISM AND *DEATH OF A SALESMAN*

The evidence for a Marxist interpretation of *Death of a Salesman* is, in any case, not very impressive. The scene in which Willy, seeking a change of job, is unceremoniously dismissed can hardly have been intended as the indictment of capitalism that Miss Clark thinks it. Theatrically it is a moving, even painful, scene, but it engenders a mixture of pity and exasperation rather than the indignation that we would expect of "party-line literature." Willy's behaviour is not calculated to enhance his or our sense of his personal dignity: even as we pity him for his despairing reduction of the wage he will settle for, we are exasperated by his inability to see that he is throwing away any chance he may have by his obtuse mishandling of Howard. The central irony of this scene resides in the discrepancy between Howard and our preconceived idea of the capitalist tycoon. This is no ruthless executive callously firing the trusted employee from calculated mercenary motives: it is the "nice guy" forced into a situation that he doesn't know how to handle "nicely" and consequently only making the ugliness of it worse. It is one little man being fired by another little man, Willy being fired by a younger Willy. Howard's callousness is occasioned less by his business acumen than by his absorption in his personal life. The tape-recorder serves two purposes in

MILLER AND MARXISM

In his autobiography, Arthur Miller describes his hearing with the House Un-American Activities Committee (HUAC). His interrogator, Richard Arens, asked Miller repeatedly to recall the organizations and causes that the playwright had supported.

The simple truth was that I myself could barely recall a great many of the organizations or causes to which I had given my support. And perhaps the worst of it all was that while these were "facts" Arens was establishing about my life as a sympathizer, it would have been impossible under the circumstances to tell the larger truth even had I been given the freedom to do so. I had indeed at times believed with passionate moral certainty that in Marxism was the hope of mankind and of the survival of reason itself, only to come up against nagging demonstrations of human perversity, not least my own. How to explain that even if he had produced a Party card with my signature on it, I could only have said yes, I had probably felt that way then, had made up my mind that day or week that the only way to stand against fascism abroad and at home was to do what so many others of my generation also thought necessary. In the plays and novels about the heroism of the Spanish Civil War and of the now long-forgotten German resistance to Hitlerism—in the whole left-wing liturgy—to be Red was to embrace hope, the hope that lies in action. So it had seemed for a time. But I have come to see an altogether different reality after traveling in the Soviet Union, particularly, and in Eastern Europe and China. Deep within Marxism, ironically enough, lies a despairing passivity before History, and indeed power is forbidden to the individual and rightfully belongs only to the collective. Thus the individual requires no rights, in the sense of protection from the state, any more than a pious person needs rights against the powers of his god. Passivity, before a revolution, derives from the belief in the Last Days whose coming no man can slow or stop; and after the revolution, from the New Law itself, which fundamentally absorbs the individual into the collective.

the scene: when Willy stumbles against it and sets it acciden-
tally into motion it precipitates an hysterical breakdown that
symbolises the central theme of the play in Willy's horror at his
inability to switch it off—to switch off the recorded past.
Whether the past is that of his own sons recorded on his memory and conscience, or that of Howard's son recorded on a mechanical instrument, it is the past, more than capitalism, of
which Willy is always the victim. The machine also provides a
means of dramatising Howard's ingenuous pride in his children. They are far more real to him than is the memory of his
father to which Willy constantly appeals, and his pride in their
prowess and their affection for him obliterates any understanding of Willy's plight, exactly as Willy's pride in his sons
has blinded him to any recognition of the worth of Bernard.
This point is emphasised by Howard's automatic question,
"Why don't your sons give you a hand ?" and by the immediate introduction of the Ben-*motif* as a further reproach to
Willy's vacillatory sentimentality. Moreover, this memory-
sequence dissolves into the actuality of Charley's office, where
a successful Bernard on his way to professional and social triumphs in Washington unintentionally prompts Willy into another orgy of envious recrimination at everybody except himself. The irony set in motion in Howard's office culminates in
Charley's, for it is Charley, not Howard, who is the nearest
thing to the big business-man in this play, and yet Charley is
the only person who offers Willy any positive help. The money
he advances him and the employment he offers have no
strings attached: Willy's acceptance of the one and rejection of
the other is the outcome of a very curious sense of personal
dignity, but there is no mistaking the truth of his exit line:

> WILLY [*on the verge of tears*]: Charley, you're the only friend I
> got. Isn't that a remarkable thing?

THE RELATIONSHIP OF WILLY AND CHARLEY

It is remarkable to Willy not only because he has never had
any time for Charley, but because Charley is the exact antithesis of himself. To describe Charley as the Horatio to Willy's
Hamlet (as one critic at least has done) is to put it too roman-
tically, but the antithesis is clearly and succinctly drawn by
Willy's exchange with Charley over Bernard's success:

> WILLY: And you never told him what to do, did you? You never
> took any interest in him.
>
> CHARLEY: My salvation is that I never took any interest in any-

thing. There's some money—fifty dollars. I got an accountant inside.

Charley the successful business-man is the only person who understands Willy the failed salesman, but he understands him in a wholly unsentimental way quite different from the "interest" that is Willy's more characteristic response. He will help Willy with a job or with money, but he will not tell him what to do: he expects Willy, like Bernard, to make his own choice. Having subordinated sentiment to business efficiency all his life, Charley can allow his feelings to come through at Willy's funeral, and his final speech, "Nobody dast blame this man . . . ," though it is not the moral of the play, ought to have made unnecessary Miller's prefatory disavowal of any intended arraignment of big business.

This tacit acceptance of business as long as it is kept distinct from sentiment is not a noticeably Marxist position. Yet Miller does not seem to intend a criticism of Howard for dismissing Willy ("When a man gets old you fire him, you have to, he can't do the work."): but he contrives that dismissal so as to show Howard in as un-business-like a light as possible. The way in which Lawrence Newman is fired in *Focus*, on far more slender grounds, makes a marked contrast to this scene. Newman is being efficiently sacrificed to business efficiency where Willy, himself a bungler, is being dismissed by a man no better than himself. To this extent we sympathise with Willy's dilemma, but our respect is not given to either party, and the dramatic impact of this scene, properly played, ought to be one of inevitability—neither has any real alternative—and of little-ness—neither is himself big enough to see the other, or to transcend his own sentimentality. Even Willy's eulogy of old Dave Singleman, who "was eighty-four years old, and he'd drummed merchandise in thirty-one states," and who "died the death of a salesman," has to be seen, for all its subdued eloquence, in this light. Strategically placed in this key scene, it constitutes a criticism of Willy in its garrulous irrelevance to this situation, and at the same time it is a condemnation of Howard for his failure to grasp its significance for Willy. Yet how little even this really means to Willy is ironically underlined in the next scene, when, tempted by Ben's offer of Alaskan wealth, he needs to be reminded of it by Linda:

BEN: What are you building? Lay your hand on it. Where is it?

WILLY [*hesitantly*]: That's true, Linda, there's nothing.

LINDA: Why? [*To Ben*] There's a man eighty-four years old. . . .

WILLY: That's right, Ben, that's right. When I look at that man
I say, what is there to worry about?

Ben's contemptuous "Bah!" is well-merited by the aura that
this has of a piece of family folk-lore, a germ of Willy's self-
deception to which Linda has been so repeatedly exposed
that she has caught the infection worse than he has.

Consumerism in *Death of a Salesman*

Michael Spindler

The rapid industrial and economic expansion of post–World War II America increased the number and affordability of consumer goods. Driven by suburban living, the acquisition of goods, and advertising, salesmen increased their sales by building relationships with people rather than promoting the goods they offered. Michael Spindler argues that this change placed a great value on assessing one's worth through the eyes of society. Willy and his sons, searching for affirmation from others, feel like they have lost their direction, their identity, and their place in society.

Spindler maintains that Ben, Dave Singleman, and Willy represent three phases of American economic change. Ben represents an early phase where a rugged individualist could compete and, if he were strong enough, rise to riches in laissez-faire capitalism. Dave Singleman represents a newer phase of consumerism where a man of personality could win friends and success in personalized, local markets. Willy, who desires to emulate Dave Singleman, is caught in a changing sales world of urbanized, anonymous mass markets. Spindler writes that in this world Willy, who is validated by the external values of prestige and public image, is victimized, alienated, and self-negated.

Michael Spindler is a lecturer in American literature at Kuwait University, Safat, Kuwait. He writes short stories and contributes articles and reviews to numerous journals and newspapers.

With the end of the Second World War, after being held in check by the 1930s recession and the imperatives of war production, the consumption-oriented phase of the American economy surged forward once more. Fuelled at first by large

Reprinted from *American Literature and Social Change*, by Michael Spindler. Copyright © 1983 by Michael Spindler. Used by permission of Macmillan Press Ltd.

personal savings accumulated during the war years, the consumer boom of the late 1940s established those features of a consumer society which emerged during the 1920s on a much larger scale. Automobile and consumer durable sales expanded at an enormous rate, as did consumer credit and advertising. Recruitment into white-collar occupations and the service trades continued to increase, as selling became a pervasive activity directly involving over three million people, some 38 per cent of whom were mobile salesmen.

Arthur Miller, in the 'Introduction' to his *Collected Plays*, speaks of his responsiveness to social change and of its shaping effect upon his art, and his *Death of a Salesman* (1949) seems especially at grips with the human problems of psychology and ideology thrown up by consumerism in the post-war period. He speaks, too, in his 'Introduction' of his shifting choice of forms according to the themes he wished to communicate, and the shift from the well-executed realism of *All My Sons* to the more expressionist mode of *Salesman* reflects Miller's awareness of, and desire to present, a new, historically conditioned consciousness. 'I wished to create a form', he wrote, 'which, in itself, as a form, would literally be the process of Willy Loman's way of mind', and in accordance with this subjectivist emphasis the set has only token representational aims. Miller has always been concerned with the interpenetration of personal and social existence, and through the interiorised structure of *Salesman* he was able to convey the heightened intensity of that interpenetration during the post-war period. Then, the psychological dimension of social life seemed to gain especial importance. The growth of white-collar personnel matched an increase in work which involved handling people rather than materials. A lifestyle of suburban residence and consumer hedonism led to an emphasis on personal wants and their gratification. Those wants were exploited and the consumer's mind manipulated by advertising. The spirit of independence and self-reliance declined and a hierarchical status system created an anxiety-producing interpersonal assessment of social worth. The dominant social values and the individual's sense of himself were interrelated in an intimate manner and D*eath of a Salesman* explores the destructive effects upon one vulnerable man of that relationship.

In *All My Sons* the main action hinged upon the intensity of a father-son relationship and demonstrated the loss of moral integrity that accompanies a dedication to a business ethic. In the doctor, Jim Bayliss, Miller reinforces this theme by presenting a minor character who has lost his best self because of a compromise with material values. 'And now I live in the usual darkness,' Jim tells Kate, 'I can't find myself; it's even hard sometimes to remember the kind of man I wanted to be.' This theme of the loss of direction and the search for identity is brought to the fore in *Salesman* and centred on a similarly intense father-son relationship.

THE SENSE OF ESTRANGEMENT IN *DEATH OF A SALESMAN*

Made aware from the beginning of a tension between Willy Loman and his son, Biff, it is not until near the play's end that we learn its root cause: Biff's discovery seventeen years before of Willy in a Boston hotel bedroom with a strange woman. The event was traumatic for them both. Willy lost his moral authority as a father and was filled with repressed guilt, and Biff from that time on could never see him as anything but a 'fake'. Their estrangement from each other and their search for some relatedness embody in their uniquely personal predicament their estrangement from themselves and their search for relatedness with the larger society.

Having lost faith in his father, Biff himself becomes 'lost', as though he never grew beyond the 17-year-old who flunked math and found that his father was not a paragon of family virtue. He seems fixated at an adolescent stage of development. 'I'm like a boy,' he tells Happy, 'I'm not married, I'm not in business, I just—I'm like a boy.' He has taken to the aimless life of the migrant worker, a life of low status and low wages, rather than the career ladder of college and business which Willy had hoped for him. This choice was partly motivated out of rebellion against the draining routine of office work and commercial standards of success, but Biff still suffers from a degree of inner conflict and his rejection of those standards is far from complete. At the play's beginning his own impulses and attempts at self-identification are still under partial subjugation to the attitudes conditioned in him by his father, and although he has returned to the city, the locus of commercial opportunity and metropolitan notions of success, he remains confused. 'I don't know—what I'm supposed to want,' he confesses in ethical bewilderment. Biff's confusion, however, is but a faint echo of Willy's own perplexity.

BEN AS A REPRESENTATIVE OF
EARLY AMERICAN INDUSTRIALISM

Willy's life has been dominated by two images of success: that of Dave Singleman which has governed its direction, and that of Ben which returns at crucial moments to highlight Willy's sense of inadequacy and insecurity. In Willy's family history we are offered a cameo of social change in America, from the pioneering father who drove his waggon and horses westward across the continent, to the elder brother who gained a fortune in the great outdoors, and finally to the travelling salesman hemmed in by the towering tenement blocks of the modern big city. 'Success incarnate', Willy calls Ben, and in Willy's image of him he becomes a caricature of success, exaggerated and simplified as Willy's mind would like success to be. Ben possesses the stern individualism and ruthless competitive spirit of the stereotyped entrepreneur. 'Never fight fair with a stranger, boy,' he instructs Biff. 'You'll never get out of the jungle that way.' 'Jungle' is used here, of course, as the stock Social Darwinian metaphor for the city under *laissez-faire* capitalism, and Charley's closely allied remarks about business competition recall Willy's protest near the beginning of the play that 'the competition is maddening!' Willy, it is evident, is not tough enough for the business struggle while Ben is. For all his urge to success Willy remains one of the exploited, a victim, while Ben is one of the exploiters. As the representative of the pioneer and entrepreneur, Ben embodies the avenues to success of the earlier, more individualistic, production phase of the American economy.

SINGLEMAN AS A REPRESENTATIVE
OF A NEW CONSUMER ECONOMY

Willy elevates him into a father-figure but he is incapable of taking his advice or following his example. Ben's appearance in Act II signifies Willy's memory of his lost opportunity when, offered a challenging job in Alaska, he chose instead security, urban life, selling. 'You've a new continent on your doorstep, William', Ben tells him, urging him to adopt an aggressive pioneering attitude. 'Get out of these cities, they're full of talk and time payments and courts of law. Screw on your fists and you can fight for a fortune up there.' But as the interview with Howard Wagner immediately before Ben's appearance alerts us, Willy had already opted for Dave Singleman and the salesman ideal of success in a consumer society:

> And old Dave, he'd go up to his room, y'understand, put on his green velvet slippers—I'll never forget—and pick up his phone and call the buyers, and without ever leaving his room, at the age of eighty-four, he made his living. And when I saw that, I realized that selling was the greatest career a man could want.

Willy counters Ben's competitive individualism with a naive faith in the power of personal attractiveness as the new Way to Wealth in the highly personalised consumer economy: 'It's who you know and the smile on your face! It's contacts, Ben, contacts! . . . a man can end with diamonds here on the basis of being liked.' Willy has based his life on the credo, 'Be liked and you'll never want', so abandoning that self-reliance embodied in Ben and represented by his father. As he becomes increasingly conscious of the failure of that credo, the image of Ben haunts him with the possibility of what he might have been.

Willy chose the pre-eminent activity of the consumer phase—selling, and so negative is the impression of salesmanship fostered by Willy's disintegration that it is easy to forget that he was drawn to it by the prospect of genuinely human, if finally illusory, rewards: 'Cause what could be more satisfying than to be able to go, at the age of eighty-four, into twenty or thirty different cities, and pick up a phone, and be remembered and loved and helped by so many different people?' Unfortunately, the personal, local markets and friendly contacts of Dave Singleman's days and Willy's own early career have given way under the pressure of urbanisation to the large, anonymous mass market, and nobody in New England knows him any more. But since Willy accepts the ideology of selling so wholeheartedly, the superficial values inculcated by salesmanship have a debilitating effect upon his character.

WILLY'S ALIENATION

In selling, the presentation of personality is all-important, since the salesman can best sell his product by impressing the buyer, by winning his confidence and trust, by making himself likeable, by selling himself. (When asked what Willy was selling, Miller writes that he could only reply 'Himself'.)

This emphasis gives rise to a character orientation which Erich Fromm, writing at the same time as *Salesman*, called the 'marketing orientation'. A salesman, like Willy, is not concerned with the attainment of some objective achievement but with the creation of a pleasing personality that will be saleable, and since he is trying to sell himself, he experiences his qualities and abilities as commodities estranged from him. This self-alienation has serious consequences, as David Riesman, following Fromm, points out. It diminishes the individual's sense of a hard core of self and, consequently, the externalised values of prestige and public image become substitutes for a genuine feeling of identity. For it is not the genuine self that is put in the market for economic success but the cosmetic self that is free from any non-saleable idiosyncrasies. When this artificial self succeeds, Riesman suggests, doubts about the loss of identity may be quieted, but since self-evaluation has been surrendered to the market, failure in the market will be translated by the individual into self-contempt. Miller indicates through Willy's frequent self-contradiction that he has no personal centre, a fact which Biff confirms when he says that Willy has no character. Willy has seized upon the notion of commercial success as a substitute for genuine identity, and when he begins to fail in the market he translates this failure into self-contempt and insecurity:

> WILLY: Oh, I'll knock 'em dead next week. I'll go to Hartford. I'm very well liked in Hartford. You know, the trouble is, Linda, people don't seem to take to me.
>
> LINDA: Oh, don't be foolish.
>
> WILLY: I know it when I walk in. They seem to laugh at me.

Since the salesman experiences himself as a commodity, he will inevitably experience others in the same way and assess their worth according to their success in the market. Thus Biff is a 'lazy bum' on this basis because his farm jobs lack status and he has yet to bring home thirty-five dollars a week.

WILLY'S ROLE AS A FATHER

Willy's main idea in bringing up his sons was not to instil moral principles in them, as a nineteenth-century Puritan-minded parent might have done, but rather to encourage them to depend upon their personal attractiveness and so equip themselves for successful careers in selling. Willy's emphasis on being 'well liked' and his dependence on others' approval distinguish him as an other-directed person. More accurately, he is an other-directed 'adjusted' person who is in the process of becoming 'anomic'. A person who has the appropriate character for his time and place is 'adjusted' even when he makes mistakes and deviates from what is expected of him. But 'utter conformity in behavior may be purchased by the individual at so high a price as to lead to character neurosis and anomie: the anomic person tends to sabotage either himself or his society.' This, together with some other remarks of Riesman and his co-workers, seems particularly apposite to Willy's personal crisis: 'The anomics include not only those who, in their character, were trained to attend to signals that are either no longer given or no longer spell meaning or success. They also may be . . . those who are overadjusted, who listen too assiduously to signals from within or without.' Willy seems to share the features of both categories. He trained himself to be a certain type of salesman that has been overtaken by social change, and so he no longer receives those signals that indicate meaning or success. Also, he seems overadjusted, especially sensitive to signals both from without—others' reactions—and from within—his anxieties and fear of failure, as the interiorised form emphasises. Finally, of course, he does 'sabotage' himself. . . .

In general terms we can recognise that while Joe Keller of *All My Sons* belonged to the old middle class and possessed the independence and secure, if limited, viewpoint of the self-made man, Willy Loman is situated in the new middle class of white-collar employees who are dependent upon others for their livelihood, values and self-esteem. Miller's shift of sociological focus demonstrates his awareness of the growing importance of this rapidly expanding occupational group. It was establishing the general texture of American social life and bringing to the fore problems associated with the discontinuity of social change such as the need for new modes of identity and new values in a greatly altered environment. Miller presents Willy in all his social relations—as employee, as erring husband, as failed father, as less successful brother, as modern consumer harassed by mortgage payments, insurance premiums and credit instalments on machines that suffer from in-built obsolescence. He is thus shown being victimised both in his capacity as worker and his capacity as consumer. Two major ironies present themselves in Willy's commitment to bourgeois values: first, he does not become a property-owner until after his death, and secondly, as a failure in selling, as a cast-off functionary in the distribution system, he is worth more dead than alive. Since he has only ever obtained monetary reward at the cost of self-negation, there is a perverse logic in his receiving the highest financial reward for his most extreme act of self-negation. . . .

Expressionism in *Death of a Salesman*

Brian Parker

In this excerpt Brian Parker describes how Arthur
Miller uses both realistic and non-realistic elements
in *Death of a Salesman*. Parker claims that the playwright blends realistic images of modern American
life—cars, aspirin, refrigerators, etc.—with symbolism and expressionism. Parker explains that Ben's
character is an important clue to Miller's expressionism. Ben is not real, rather he is an expression of
Willy's desire for escape and success. The play's expressionism is partially established by the setting as
well, originally designed by Jo Mielziner, which uses
a skeletal house framework, sketchy furnishings,
colored lighting, and sounds and music to move the
audience deep into the mind and memory of Willy
Loman. Ultimately, Miller's expressionistic techniques force the audience members to become Willy
Lomans for the duration of the play, allowing them
to see and feel as Willy does.

Brian Parker teaches American literature and
drama at Trinity College, University of Toronto.

The realism in *Death of a Salesman* is fairly obvious, and reflects the influence on Miller of Henrik Ibsen, the Ibsen, that
is, of the middle phase, the great realist reformer. In *All My
Sons* and *Death of a Salesman* Miller adopts Ibsen's "retrospective" structure, in which an explosive situation in the
present is both explained and brought to a crisis by the gradual revelation of something which has happened in the past:
in *Death of a Salesman* this is, of course, Willy Loman's adultery, which by alienating his son, Biff, has destroyed the
strongest value in Willy's life. This structure is filled out with
a detailed evocation of modern, urban, lower-middle class

Reprinted with the permission of Simon and Schuster from Brian Parker, "Point of
View in Arthur Miller's *Death of a Salesman*, in *Twentieth-Century Interpretations of
"Death of a Salesman,"* edited by Helene Wickham Koon. Copyright © 1983 by
Prentice-Hall, Inc.

life: Miller documents a world of arch-supports, aspirin, spectacles, subways, time payments, advertising, Chevrolets, faulty refrigerators, life insurance, mortgages, and the adulation of high school football heroes. The language, too, except in a few places which will be considered later, is an accurate record of the groping, half inarticulate, cliché-ridden inadequacy of ordinary American speech. And the deadly realism of the picture is confirmed for us by the way that American audiences have immediately recognized and identified with it in the theatre.

SYMBOLIC REALISM IN THE PLAY

However, even in his realist plays, Ibsen has details which, while still being acceptably probable, have also a deeper, symbolic significance: one thinks of such things as the polluted swimming baths in *The Enemy of the People*, the eponymous wild duck, or, more abstractly, the hair and pistols motifs in *Hedda Gabler*. Such a deepening of realism is also a technique in *Death of a Salesman*. Consider, for instance, the value that Willy and his sons attach to manual work, and its glamorous extension, sport, their belief that it is necessary for a man to keep fit, to be able to handle tools and build things. Willy's handiness around the house is constantly impressed on us: "He was always good with his hands," Linda remembers, and Biff says that his father put more enthusiasm into building the stoop than into all his salesmanship; in his reveries Willy again teaches his boys how to simonize a car the most efficient way, and is contemptuous of his neighbour Charlie, and Charlie's son Bernard, because they lack the manual skills; Willy's favourite son, Biff, is even more dextrous than his father—in high school he was a star athlete and, as a man, he can find happiness only as a ranch hand; one remembers that Willy's father was a pioneer type who drove over the country in a wagon, earning money by ingenious inventions and the making of flutes. Willy's mystique of physical skill is thus a reflection of the simpler, pioneer life he craves, a symptom and a symbol of his revolt against the constraints of the modern city.

Slightly more abstract, yet still realistic, is the play's use of trees to symbolize the rural way of life which modern commercialism is choking. Willy, we are told, bought his house originally because it stood in a wooded suburb where he could hunt a little, and where his yard was flanked by two great elms; but now the trees have been cut down and his property is so over-shadowed by apartment houses that he cannot even grow seed in his back garden. (The choked seed is a fairly obvious symbol: Willy Loman is trapped in a society which prevents him establishing anything to outlast himself, ruining the lives of his sons as well as his own.) We learn at the beginning that it is dreaming about the countryside and watching scenery, particularly trees, which is the main cause of Willy's recent road accidents; it is to look after timber that Willy's brother, Ben, tries to persuade him to go to Alaska; the "jungle" Ben says, is the place for riches; and at moments of crisis Willy yells "The woods are burning," a phrase which is nonsensical unless seen in context of the other tree references.

The last example is already diverging from realism: that is, it is not a phrase habitually used in American life; it needs the context of the play to give it meaning. And when we find Miller directing that, whenever Willy remembers the past, the stage be drenched in a green, checkered pattern of leaves, then it is obvious that the technique has moved from realistic symbolism to outright expressionism.

JO MIELZINER'S EXPRESSIONISTIC SET

The set for the play, designed by Jo Mielziner but to Miller's specifications, and influenced, no doubt, by the set for O'Neill's *Desire under the Elms*, is a bizarre but wholly successful mingling of realism and non-realism. Its skeletal house shows several rooms simultaneously (like mediaeval staging); the house is sparsely furnished with just enough properties to suggest a sense of place and environment, with the result, as the first stage direction suggests, that "an air of dream clings to the place, a dream rising out of reality"; and the house has in front of it a bare, neutral forestage, used (as in the Elizabethan theatre) to represent any place demanded by the story, with necessary props being carried on and off by the characters themselves. The skeletal framework of the house also gives it a sense of fragility which is intensified by surrounding it with the menacing silhouettes of tall apartment houses, producing an effect of claustrophobia, of rural wood menaced by asphalt jungle.

The set is expressionistically lit to reinforce this impression. The apartment silhouettes are bathed in angry orange; when Willy remembers the past, the house is dappled by the green of vanished trees; when Biff and Hap pick up two women and neglect their father, the directions request a lurid red; and at the end, when Willy insanely tries to plant seed by night, the "blues" of the stage direction simultaneously suggests moonlight and his mood of despair. Music is similarly manipulated: the rural way of life is represented by flute music, telling "of grass and trees and the horizon"; it is heard only by Willy whenever he dreams of the life he should have led or of the early days when his suburb was still in the country. It is associated, of course, with Willy's pioneer father, the flute maker; and in the modern world has degenerated to Willy and Biff's unbusinesslike habit of whistling in elevators, and, at a yet further remove, to the mechanized whistling of Howard and his children as played back on a tape recorder. The tape recorder scene is, in fact, a brilliantly compact piece of symbolism, functioning like the "mirror scene" in some of Shakespeare's plays (or Brecht's "*Grundgestus*") to epitomize the action of the whole play: not only does it illustrate the mechanization of family life, but Howard's idolizing of his children and bullying of his wife exactly parallel Willy's, showing a resemblance between the two men which undercuts left-wing clichés about employer and worker; and, when Willy knocks it over and cannot stop it, the machine serves as both cause and illustration of Willy's mental breakdown: he has one of his schizophrenic attacks, and the mechanical voices, so like those of his own home life, are an equivalent to the clamorous subconscious of which he has also lost control. The crucial hotel bedroom scene, in which Biff discovers his father's adultery, is heralded by a shrill trumpet blast, and Willy's final disaster is conveyed by musical shorthand: his decision to commit suicide is accompanied by a prolonged, maddening note, which collapses into a crash of discords, to represent the car crash offstage, and then modulates into a dead march to introduce the requiem scene. Certain characters and situations also have what amount to *leit-motifs*: besides the flute music, we are told there is a 'boys musical'; raucous sex music for the scene of Biff's discovery and the barroom scene where Biff and Hap pick up women; and a special music to herald the appearances in Willy's memory of his elder brother, Ben.

BEN AS AN EXPRESSIONISTIC CHARACTER

The presentation of Ben is an important clue as to exactly how, and why, Miller is using expressionism in *Death of a*

Salesman. He is distinctly less "real" than the other characters of the play, stiffer, with a more stilted way of speaking: in
the original production, Elia Kazan had the part acted unnat-
urally, like an automaton. Ben seems less "real" than the others because he is not so much a person as the embodiment
of Willy's desire for escape and success: Willy calls him "success incarnate." This is proved by the fact that he does not
only appear in memory scenes but is summoned up at the
end to "discuss" Willy's plan of suicide; obviously, he here
represents a side of Willy's own mind. It is interesting to note,
therefore, that the stage directions emphasize that Ben always appears at exactly the moment Willy thinks of him,
which is not true of the other characters in the memory
scenes. The figure of Ben, then, represents not Ben as he actually was, so much as Ben as his image has been warped in
the mind of the rememberer, Willy; and this reveals the peculiar nature of expressionism in *Death of a Salesman.*

WILLY'S MEMORIES

Miller is not using expressionistic techniques in the way they
are used by the German writers of the 1920's, to dramatize
abstract forces in politics or economics or history. He is using
the techniques solely as a means of revealing the character of
Willy Loman, the values Willy holds and, particularly, the
way his mind works. Miller's reason for blending realism
and expressionism in *Death of a Salesman* is that this combination reflects the protagonist's actual way of thinking: "I
wished to create a form," says Miller, "which . . . would literally be the process of Willy Loman's mind." It is Willy Loman's character, therefore, which is the chief link between
the two dramatic modes, and this is possible, of course, because Willy is technically a schizophrenic: overwork, worry
and, particularly, repressed guilt have resulted in a mental
breakdown in which present and past mingle for him inextricably, where, in Miller's own phrase, time is "exploded."

As Miller points out, this is not a "flashback" technique (the
film of *Death of a Salesman* failed precisely because it tried to
turn the memory sequences into flashbacks); what it does is
to present a past distorted by the rememberer's mind—a subjective, not objective record; and the memories have an extra
tension because they occur simultaneously with events in the
present, more like a double exposure than a flashback. Note,
for instance, how the memory scenes appear gradually,

usurping the present bit by bit in the card game with Charlie when Willy is talking to the remembered Ben and the actual Charlie simultaneously, or the gradual emergence of the repressed hotel bedroom scene which is brought to a climax when Biff's and Happy's pick-ups enter in the present. This simultaneous presentation of past and present, dream and reality, gives the play a metaphoric quality, a Cocteau-ish [French writer, Jean Cocteau] "poetry of the theatre," which (in my opinion) compensates for the so often criticized banality of language. Ambiguity, irony, and tension occur in the action and stage pictures, not in the wording where they might, more conventionally, be expected. It is a metaphor in time.

THE PLAY'S FORM

The form of the play, then, depends on the gradual admission by Willy *to himself* of his own guilt; it differs from the public exposés of Ibsen's form in that Willy's adultery is never openly discussed between him and Biff, and Linda and Hap never learn of it at all: the sole importance is that Willy himself should recognize it. Normal chronology is ignored, therefore: the order of events depends on the way that memories of the past swim up out of Willy's memory because of their emotional association with things happening in the present. For example, Willy's worry about having nearly crashed his car in the present brings up memories of happy experiences with cars in the past; as Willy eases his feeling of inferiority to Charlie by mocking Charlie's lack of skill with tools, this conjures up the memory of Ben, Willy's ideal of practical success, and leads with emotional but not chronological logic to reminiscences of their pioneer father. Note, particularly, that certain things always "trigger" this kind of mental relapse in Willy because they are so associated with his guilt: silk stockings, for instance, or the sound of women laughing; and the blurring of mental realities is represented visually by characters stepping across the wall lines of the skeletal setting. Miller says: ". . . the structure of the play was determined by what was needed to draw up [Willy's] memories like a mass of tangled roots without end or beginning." This provides a sense of climax because "if I could make him remember enough he would kill himself."

However, Miller's explanation of his purpose fails to account for an important inconsistency in the use of expressionism. The play does not divide neatly into realistic scenes in the present and expressionistic memory scenes in Willy's mind; some of the expressionistic scenes deal with events in the present when Willy is not even there, and cannot therefore be said to be distorted through his schizophrenia. Consider the scenes downtown in Howard's office or the barroom, before Willy arrives, which are represented nonrealistically on the unlocalized forestage; or, most strikingly, the unrealism of the "Requiem" scene, where characters break the wall lines to come downstage, and the forestage itself represents a graveyard. This cannot be a distortion of Willy's mind because Willy is already dead.

The rationale behind the mingling of realism and expressionism is thus uncertain. The result is intriguing. The extension of expressionism to non-memory scenes means that we see even events which Willy did not experience as though through Willy's eyes, as Willy might have experienced them. The play's technique thus forces the audience to become Willy Lomans for the whole duration of the play, to sympathize with his predicament in a way they could not do in real life. It allows them to see more than Willy does, but not to see more than he might have seen; they are expected to criticize Willy, but the technique forces them to criticize him from within, as Willy criticizes and condemns himself. Miller tells us some interesting facts about the genesis of the play which are relevant here:

> The first image that occurred to me which was to result in *Death of a Salesman* was an enormous face to the height of the proscenium arch which would appear and then open up, and we would see the inside of a man's head. In fact, *The Inside of His Head* was the first title. It was conceived half in laughter, for the inside of his head was a mass of contradictions.

The last sentence is particularly important because it reflects on the values of the play in a way which has not yet been analysed: if we see *all* the play as Willy might have experienced it, even those scenes in which he does not actually appear, then all the values of the play, good as well as bad, will be restricted to values which Willy might himself have held. The frame of values will be relative to the potential of a character like Willy's, adjusted to the limits of his imagination. This important "point of view" in the play has been invariably neglected: discussions of *Death of a Salesman* assume that it presents Miller's own values, and Miller's defense of Willy as a tragic hero has done nothing to rectify the error.

Society and Home in *Death of a Salesman*

Irving Jacobson

Irving Jacobson maintains that one constant thematic element running through Miller's plays, including *Death of a Salesman*, is the driving need for characters to transform an impersonal social world into a place of familial warmth, safety, and honor. Willy believes that this can be achieved by gaining prominence through wealth and business success.

Jacobson examines the methods that Ben, Dave Singleman, and Biff use to connect with the outside world: Ben commands wealth and power to place himself above the need for family or society's positive response; Singleman relates to society by enmeshing himself in social relationships and public love; and Biff, before he drops out of society, evokes affection with a godlike or heroic status. According to Jacobson, all three are mythological for Willy and, as such, remain a mystery to him. Willy can't crack the code to transform society into a home and the result is loneliness and frustration. When the Loman family reunites in the play, the hope for family unity crumbles and the separation between family members is sealed.

Irving Jacobson works and teaches at Upstate Medical Center, State University of New York, Syracuse.

[Literary critic] Robert Hogan has noted that much of Miller's work developed from the image of man "struggling to be at one with society." Miller elucidates the nature of this struggle in "The Family in Modern Drama," where he finds all great drama to be concerned with some aspect of a single problem: "How may a man make of the outside world a

Excerpted from Irving Jacobson, "Family Dreams in *Death of a Salesman,*" *American Literature*, vol. 47, no. 2 (May 1975), pp. 247–58. Copyright 1975, Duke University Press. Reprinted with permission.

home?" What does he need to do, to change within himself or in the external world, if he is to find "the safety, the surroundings of love, the ease of soul, the sense of identity and honor which, evidently, all men have connected in their memories with the idea of family?" This concern remains a constant in Miller's work. He is quoted in *Psychology and Arthur Miller* by Richard I. Evans as observing that his own sense of drama resides in the emotional tension within a person drawn to the past in order to orient himself to the present. His characters feel displaced from what they should be, even from what they "really" are. Although Miller does not make explicit reference here to childhood and the family, the sense of radical loss and the passionate need to reattain some previous and necessary state seem fundamentally the same as in "The Family in Modern Drama."

With the success of *All My Sons*, wrote Miller, "It suddenly seemed that the audience was a mass of blood relations and I sensed a warmth in the world that was not there before." He attributed success to the power to transform a relatively impersonal social world into a home that offered familial warmth. His next play, probably the most stunning portrayal of failure in the American theatre, dramatized a man's inability to achieve this transformation. Nothing Loman says or does can evoke that "warmth in the world." Instead, society responds to him with an indifference that can only seem cruel in juxtaposition to the hopes he carries with him even to the point of death.

Loman articulates his need in appealing to his employer with an image of the past, a Golden Age: "In those days there was personality in it, Howard. There was respect, and comradeship and gratitude in it. Today it's all cut and dried, and there's no chance for bringing friendship to bear—or personality." Earlier Miller characters found these values outside the business world: Gus in the Merchant Marine, in *The Story of Gus;* Chris Keller in the Army, in *All My Sons*. Loman once found them in having coffee with the mayor of Providence, in being recognized in places like Slattery's, Filene's, and the Hub, and by enjoying such good standing with New England policemen that he could park his car anywhere he liked without getting a ticket. His sense of self-value, then, depended upon the response of others. Such gestures of recognition provided signals that society, for a period in his life, was a home for him, one where he might hope to make his sons as happily at ease as he.

Prominence, whether gained through wealth, business associations, or public esteem, appeared to be the major catalyst in turning the world's indifference into warmth and admiration. Loman expressed awe at the prominence of Thomas Edison, B.F. Goodrich, and Frank Wagner, but the most compelling images of success were Ben, Dave Singleman, and Biff. The entrepreneur, the renowned salesman, and the star high school athlete represented possibilities in life to which Loman could not attain. They were surrounded men. At school, Biff was surrounded by admiring classmates and, at the Ebbets Field game, by cheering crowds and brilliant sunlight. At the peak of his career and at the end of his life, Singleman was surrounded by the affection of customers and fellow salesmen.

BEN'S RELATIONSHIP WITH SOCIETY

Ben, however, was surrounded by the mystery and power of his enterprising audacity. He represented a way of being at home in the world that differed from Miller's statement about the public response to *All My Sons* and from the attainments of other successful characters in *Death of a Salesman*. The world was a home for Ben not by the affection he won from it but by the command of his wealth, power, and mobility. In the world of finance he was as much a pioneer, a "great and wild-hearted man," as his father. His imagination and life extended as easily to Alaska, South Dakota, and Africa as to New York. Apparently indifferent to social relationships, he needed neither the human warmth of the family nor society's positive response. His sphere of action related to things and quantities rather than people; even his seven sons seemed more like commodities than members of a family. Thereby the play implies, not without irony, Ben was more capable of becoming at ease in the world than Willy Loman, whose refusal to join with his brother, a choice rooted in an ethic oriented to the family and to society, signaled his financial, social and family failures.

DAVE SINGLEMAN'S RELATIONSHIP WITH SOCIETY

The world became a home for Dave Singleman in an opposite fashion. Like Ben, he enjoyed wealth, power and mobility; but these were more entirely enmeshed within social relationships. The nature and extent of his prominence was succinctly illustrated in his ability to sit in a hotel room and make his living by phone, comfortably attired in the luxury of green velvet slippers. This image has had a decisive power in Loman's life:

> And when I saw that, I realized that selling was the greatest career a man could want. 'Cause what could be more satisfying than to be able to go, at the age of eighty-four, into twenty or thirty different cities, and pick up a phone, and be remembered and loved and helped by so many different people?

Unlike Ben, Singleman achieved a success that presented him with a world of loyalty, aid, and love. His scope of action was spatially more limited in being national rather than international; but response to him was more personal. For Loman, the surest indication of public love for Singleman is that when he died the "death of a salesman" in the smoking car of a train on the way to Boston, people travelled from all over the country to attend his funeral. In juxtaposition to Loman's funeral in the "Requiem" of the play, this reveals the extent to which Singleman's prominence granted him a home in society that Loman cannot achieve. Singleman mastered his society not through the demonic qualities one perceives in Ben but through a synthesis of man's social and economic impulses.

BIFF'S RELATIONSHIP WITH SOCIETY

The world became a home for Biff Loman when, as an athlete, he evoked affection and admiration from the people around him. His life seemed full of promise, with a choice of three college scholarships to signify the abundance of future success life can offer the already successful. When he became captain of the football team, a crowd of girls surrounded him after classes, and girls paid for him on dates. His friends waited for him after school, not knowing how to occupy themselves until he arrived to organize them into sweeping out the furnace and hanging up his mother's laundry. As contrasted with his friend Bernard, who was only "liked," Biff was "well-liked," which seemed to grant him, in Loman's view, certain allowances that could not be bestowed upon those who received less fervent popular esteem. At the all-star Ebbets Field game he was the tallest player, dressed in gold with the sun all around him while the crowd shouted "Loman, Loman, Loman!" so that his father sensed him raised beyond the level of the merely human by the extent of his prominence among others.

Prominence for Ben, Singleman, and Biff has an impersonal quality that contradicts Loman's repeated insistence upon the value of personality and what he calls "personal attractiveness." His heroes tend to stand among yet above other people. He remarks that at the Ebbets Field game Biff seemed like "Hercules—something like that," and his accounts of Ben's being "success incarnate" have more the tone of hagiography than family anecdote. For Loman these figures exist less as individuals with actual characters, talents, and problems than as mythological projections of his own needs and his society's values. This has two kinds of consequences for his life. For one, the means for achieving success remain a mystery to him. Although he perceives Ben as a sign that "The greatest things can happen!" he can never discover how those things happen. When he asks Ben how to succeed he receives not an answer but an incantatory formula: "When I was seventeen I walked into the jungle, and when I was twenty-one I walked out. And by God I was rich." Ben proves willing to use violence when it is necessary or useful, and he boasts of his mnemonic powers; but these cannot lead Loman to understand how Ben became wealthy, much less how anyone else might. Another consequence of Loman's mythological projection is that characters without strikingly luminous qualities, such as Charlie or Linda, cannot move Loman deeply enough to help him. Charlie's aid and friendship represent the only instance where someone in society does form something like a family tie with him. Yet Charlie can offer only help, not promise; realistic advice, not transformation. He has succeeded in business, but no aura of magic power surrounds him or his advice.

The consequences of failing to attain prominence and to transform society into a home are loneliness, frustration, and ultimately despair. Because Loman needs gratification to take a social form, his life is crushed by indifference, criticism, rejection, and abandonment. In his scene with Howard Wagner he appeals to quasi-familial ties in the past—"I was with the firm when your father used to carry you in here in his arms" —but the reality that "business is business" and not a family makes his appeal irrelevant. At the same time that Wagner's act corresponds, figuratively, to rejection by a son, it also records a final loss of hope that family ties can exist on a social level. But, still unable to accept failure in his struggle to be at one with society, Loman prefers death with the illusion of transformation to life without it. . . .

WILLY'S DESIRE FOR FAMILY UNITY

Loman wants to feel a unity of generations linking his father and Ben with him and his sons. He appeals to Ben: "You're just what I need, Ben, because I—I have a fine position here, but I—well, Dad left when I was such a baby, and I never had a chance to talk to him and I still feel—kind of temporary about myself." Yet the need for family unity is juxtaposed against the reality of family disintegration. Loman's father abandons his family, and Ben leaves soon afterward. Loman violates the unity of his family with the woman in Boston, not only by sexual infidelity but by giving her the stockings that should go to Linda. Biff leaves home because of his discovery, and Happy leaves to set up his own apartment and enjoy his women. Sex proves a powerfully divisive force among the Lomans, separating parents from each other and parents from sons. Happy abandons his father in another way, by merely sending him away to Florida when Loman's emotional breakdown becomes embarrassingly visible. He cannot respond sympathetically to his father's problems. "No, that's not my father," he dismissively remarks in the restaurant scene, "He's just a guy."

Linda remained loyal, but her constancy cannot help Loman. She can play no significant role in her husband's dreams; and although she proves occasionally capable of dramatic outbursts, she lacks the imagination and strength to hold her family together or to help Loman define a new life without grandiose hopes for Biff. Critics have attacked her as "profoundly unsatisfactory" as a character, "not in the least sexually interesting," and a symbol of the "cash-payment fixation." But given Loman's inability to accept disagreement from his sons or Charlie, it is hard to suppose that he would tolerate a less acquiescent wife. He calls her "my foundation and my support," but her stability cannot prevent his collapse.

In "The Family as a Psychosocial Organization," Robert D. Hess and Gerald Handel have noted that "The family's life together is an endless process of movement in and around consensual understanding, from attachment to conflict and withdrawal—and over again. Separateness and connectedness are the underlying conditions of a family's life, and its common task is to give form to both." In *Death of a Salesman,* beginning the process "over again" becomes impossible. The

present action of the play forces an explosive reunion, bringing members of the family together in order to make their
separateness explicit and irrevocable. This pattern typifies
Arthur Miller's work; it occurs in *All My Sons;* it character-
izes *After the Fall;* and it encompasses most of *The Price.* Attempts to recreate family unity—like Ben's offer of partner-
ship, Biff's return home, or the brothers' schemes to go into
business together—have the dual effect of illuminating areas
of conflict and forever sealing family members off from one
another. The peripatetic big dinner scene toward the end of
the play, then, presents a cacophony of dissonant motives;
and the centripetal forces of their separate lives prove
stronger than the need for unity that brought the Lomans together. Torn between Happy's callous ability to let him continue living in illusion and Biff's cruel but necessary demand for honesty, Loman yields to a hope forged in despair:
that Biff might finally recant and become "magnificent"
with the insurance money. But his death changes nothing; it
implies instead that a man's frenetic attempt to make the
world a home can defeat the viability of his private home,
even cost him his life.

The Oedipal Theme in *Death of a Salesman*

Daniel E. Schneider

Daniel E. Schneider argues that there is an inner psychological theme in *Death of a Salesman*. Miller's play portrays a variation of the Oedipal Complex when Biff rejects his father as a sexless god who can protect him from all misdemeanors and begins to see him as a sexual man, prone to temptation. Schneider suggests that the restaurant scene unfolds as a father murder when the boys abandon Willy, leaving him alone to re-live his Boston infidelity. After learning of the abandonment, Linda attacks Biff and Happy and, according to Schneider, espouses a related contemporary social theme that warns society not to destroy fatherhood because it will make criminals of the sons. Schneider goes on to explicate another major psychological theme of the play, the hatred of a younger brother toward an older one. Both Willy, a younger brother to Ben, and Happy, a younger brother to Biff, are envious and jealous of their older brothers. Both feel and act like deprived sons.

Daniel E. Schneider, M.D., had a long career in psychiatry and psychoanalysis. He was a fellow of the American Academy of Psychoanalysis; Life-Member of the American Psychiatric Association; and Director of the Foundation for Perception and Talent. His works include *The Growth Concept of Nervous Integration, The Psychoanalyst and the Artist,* and *Revolution in the Body-Mind.*

We must pursue the inner psychological theme. Willy Loman is not in the eyes of his sons just a man, but a god in decay. To his first son Biff, Willy was a god who would protect him from all misdemeanor, who could "fix" even a failure in mathematics; to his sons, Willy Loman was Salesman-Lord of New England. It is this illusion of sexless godhood that is shattered when Biff at seventeen comes to Boston on a surprise mission (to get his father to "fix" a math failure) and catches Willy with a lusty woman, then breaks down, weeps and walks out on his father who is on his knees pleading for forgiveness, understanding and lost godhood. This is the repressed scene of infidelity and smashed authority dramatized in the restaurant.

THE OEDIPUS THEME IN *DEATH OF A SALESMAN*

What theme is this? At what point does a son recognize finally and for all time that a father is not a sexless god but a sexual man, prone to every human temptation? It is a variation of the Oedipus theme, a variation which says: *he who pretends to godhood over me must fulfill his godhood or be revealed as a madman.*

Follow the second act from this point of view, and it is sheer murder of a father by "all his sons"—an irrational Oedipal blood-bath given seeming rationalization by the converging social theme of the worn-out salesman. Willy Loman is really brought low in this second act. Blow after blow descends upon him until, symbolically castrated, shouting madly he is forced to his knees, to pounding on the floor.

He is told he is no good as a salesman and never was—by his dead boss's son to whom he was godfather, whom he named. He is told by his nephew that at seventeen something happened to Biff which destroyed the boy, a hint of Willy's infidelity. At the restaurant where the feast of celebration (totem-feast) was to have taken place, he is told by Biff that Biff has just compulsively stolen the fountain pen (genital) of a man who, Willy imagined, might have started Biff on his hoped-for rehabilitation. It is at this point that the father has to rush to the bathroom—a piece of dramatic action which tells us, as explicitly as we can be told, that the father is in castration-panic; and the panic in the father is matched by the younger son's promotion of a date with two "babes." The meaning of this episode can hardly be missed. It is the ultimate act of father-murder; instead of the totem-feast in which the sons recognize the father's authority and sexual rights, there is no dinner. There is only abandonment. Emerging from the bathroom, re-living his own sexual infidelity, Willy Loman—ex-god—has no recourse but to shout in rage at the sexual assertion of the sons. And it is followed immediately by the mother's accusation against her sons for their killing their father by their whoring. This is as close to the original battle fought eons ago by man and his sons as has ever been put upon the stage. It is this very thinly and yet very adroitly disguised Oedipal murder which gives the play *its peculiar symbolic prehistoric* power. It is not only modern man exploited; it is also Neanderthal man raging against the restraint of civilization's dawn.

LINDA'S DEFENSE OF WILLY

It is from this point on that the play in its last few minutes rises to critical intensity. The external contemporary social theme (announced by the mother near the end of the first act: "Attention—attention must finally be paid to such a man!") now converges and clashes with the eon-old psychological theme of the murdering, incestuous, whoring sons. Again, as in *All My Sons*, it is the mother fighting savagely for the father as she accuses the sons; it is the mother who sets off the older son's fury. It is she who has faced with the father the agonies of salesmanship, refrigerators, mortgages, life insurance, exhaustion and withering. Her rage at being old and dried-up is implicit as she fights like a she-tiger against the sons who have cast off the father for their own sexual philandering. It is thus she who is the protagonist of the external social theme: *a society that destroys fatherhood makes primitives (criminals) of its sons.*

In the last few minutes of the play, her confronting them ignites an explosive climax which is every dramatist's ambition. Biff, the protagonist of the Oedipal theme, goes into maniacal fury at the mother's defense of the father and exposes him as a philanderer and a fake, and is about to strike the tottering Willy. Then at the very last moment, because Biff, too, has lived by now and knows how tough civilization is against dreams and hopes, at the very last moment of conflict Biff is overtaken by pity and love and falls weeping into the stunned father's arms. This is an ultimate moment of climax rarely achieved in any theatre.

SIBLING CONFLICT IN *DEATH OF A SALESMAN*

The tragedy now resolves itself powerfully upon its basic and hidden motivation: the guilt of a younger son for his hatred of his older brother, for Willy Woman is also a younger brother.

Willy reaffirms father-son love: "That boy is going to be magnificent!" he shouts, after saying incredulously, "He loves me!" But at the same time it is just this reconciliation between father and first son which must not be tolerated by the basic drive of the play. It is made to appear that Willy Loman can no longer endure this burden of fatherhood, this pity, this love of his first son, this evidence of authority which has failed, of fallen godhood. For again the repeated hallucination of *Willy's older brother Ben* appears, this time summoning Willy now to come away to new adventure (Death) in Ben's bragging, nagging refrain: "I was seventeen when I went into the jungle, and when I came out I was twenty-one and rich!" Here, in the play's final resolution, the entire necessity for the technique of hallucination becomes clear, though in fact it was announced at the very beginning of the play when Willy Loman commented that his older brother Ben, who struck it rich, is dead. Willy Loman, himself a younger brother (low-man on a totem pole), was determined in his time to "lick the system" by the magic of salesmanship and become "No. 1 Man"—a son with a deep guilty hatred for his older brother.

In this sense, the entire play has the aura of a dream, a wish of prehistoric proportion, its strength lying in its adroit social rationalization, in its superlative disguise of the role of the younger son Hap. It is as though Hap reported this dream:

"I had a strange dream last night. I dreamt that my father (who is a younger son and a salesman as I am) came home from one of his trips unable any longer to control his car. As he comes in, he is carrying two black, battered sample cases. They seem to have some ominous meaning as they weigh him down. In the dream he seems to be quite old and broken and starts shouting at my mother so loud that I and my brother Biff, who has come home from his wandering, hear him in our room upstairs where we lie sleeping. I explain to my brother that our father is losing his mind. As we listen, my father's older brother Ben, also a wanderer who struck it rich, is on my father's mind and he imagines that Ben is talking, calling to him.

"I persuade Biff to go into business with me and we plan to make good. But somehow Biff steals a fountain pen from the man who was to support our plan. (Biff used to steal, but my father let him get away with everything.) And my father plans to get a job from his boss's son, a position where he

> ### MILLER'S PSYCHOLOGICAL INTERPRETATIONS OF LITERATURE
>
> *In his book* The Writer and Psychology, *Richard Evans, a professor of psychology, asks Miller to give his opinion on using the principles of psychology in literary criticism.*
>
> I haven't read very much of what has been written about that play [*Death of a Salesman*] or any of my plays, much as I realize that a lot has been written, but what I've read about *Death of A Salesman* was mixed. . . . My personal attitude is curiosity about what psychologists make of the material, but a suspension of disbelief, so to speak; I wonder sometimes what help it is to anybody to have all those pieces of structural information, structural in the sense that they conform to a Freudian psychology or don't conform to it. It seems to me that a lot of people have gotten lost in making this analysis an end in itself. . . . My point is that I would want psychology to refer itself more and more to literature, more and more to life, rather than to refer itself back to psychology. I think there is a danger that psychology is becoming the literature, that the so-called scientific view of man and motivation is becoming the literature of the twentieth century. My point is that there is a growing tendency not only to substitute psychoanalysis or psychological analysis for art, but to regard it as the prime source of information about man, and I don't believe in it.

won't have to go on the road any more. My mother is very happy about all this because she is worried that my father is going to commit suicide. She is very happy about Biff's coming home and about his getting together with father, but pays little attention to me.

"But in the next scene of my dream, which seems to be the next day, everything goes wrong. My father is told by the boss's son, to whom my father was godfather, that he never was any good as a salesman. And the dinner we are to have with my father in a chophouse to celebrate doesn't come off, though we do meet there. It doesn't come off because nobody has succeeded—except me, because I still have my job. My father gets furious with Biff for stealing the fountain pen and Biff gets furious with my father for imagining that Biff ever could make good. Then I catch sight of a beautiful babe in the restaurant, and I tell her to get a girl friend, and Biff and I go off with the two of them to lay them all night. As we leave I seem to see my father rush into the bathroom and then come out and sink to his knees and shout and pound with his fist, something about giving Biff an order.

"In the last scene of the dream, when we get home, my mother goes into a rage and accuses us of whoring and of killing our father. Biff gets furious and begins to attack my father while I stand aside and watch, as though I were part of an audience at a play. Just as Biff is about to strike my father, he falls instead weeping into my father's arms. My father shouts: 'He loves me! . . . That boy is going to be magnificent!'

"Then Uncle Ben seems to call to my father—and this part is strange because I seem to see Ben as clearly as my father does, again as though it were a play of the inside of my father's mind. My father rushes out after Ben and gets killed by a car.

"There is a tag-end to the dream. A sad little piece. It takes place at my father's grave. My mother moans that she doesn't understand it, especially since they had just made the last payment on the mortgage. Biff says that he is going away from the city. But not I. I vow that I'm going to lick the system and be No. 1 Man. It is very sad."

This is the dream of a younger, unpreferred son. No other analysis, it seems to me, can account for the increasing frequency of the vision of Ben, Willy's older and envied brother. In a sense, every first son "strikes it rich" in a younger son's eyes.

Death of a Salesman is an enduring play. It will be performed over and over for many years, because of its author's masterful exposition of the unconscious motivations in our lives. It is one of the most concentrated expressions of aggression and pity ever to be put on the stage. If Arthur Miller's *All My Sons* was aptly named, then this work is All Our Fathers.

CHAPTER 2

Willy Loman

READINGS ON
DEATH OF A SALESMAN

Father/Son Relationships in the Play

Neil Carson

Neil Carson states that any assessment of *Death of a Salesman* must be built on an understanding of Willy's inner life. Willy has a subconscious fear that what he has been telling his boys and his wife, Linda, has not been true or decent.

Carson agrees with the critics who approach the play as a psychological drama focusing on family relationships, particularly father/son conflicts. Willy, a boy-man, stuck in adulthood as an eternal adolescent, has problems as an adult that are directly related to his deprivation as a son. Carson notes that the recurring flute music in the play recalls Willy's father who made and sold flutes. The older Loman was both a strong entrepreneur and a creative inventor who left when Willy was a young boy. Carson suggests that two sides of the father are represented in the play by Dave Singleman, an old New England salesman, and Ben, Willy's brother. Singleman is a father figure who in Willy's mind represents the success of his father and, at the same time, the success of the free enterprise system, a system that ironically does not exist. Ben, vague and ghostlike, is a father figure who represents the inventive side of Willy's father. According to Carson, Ben presents the daring which Willy admires but does not possess. Carson concludes that Willy, deprived as a child, is emotionally crippled because he can't come to terms with his father.

Neal Carson is associate professor of English at University of Guelph in Ontario, Canada.

It is the presentation of Willy's internal life which is the most striking feature of the play and the one which must be understood before a final assessment of the work can be made.

Willy's memories do not materialise at random. They are triggered by certain incidents in the present, and Willy is changed by remembering them. A detailed examination of this process is impossible, but a single example may illustrate the point. Willy's first return to the past in the play is the result of his recollection of the time when Biff seemed so full of promise. It is brought on by Biff's return home and the inevitable tension between the two men which is a consequence of Biff's apparent inability to settle down. It begins with Willy remembering his son waxing the car and proceeds to recollections of other details such as the way in which Biff 'borrowed' a football from the school locker-room. The guilt Willy felt even then about exaggerating his own accomplishments and encouraging his sons to disregard the law is suggested by the appearance of Linda in the memory.

WILLY'S SUBCONSCIOUS FEAR

Since Willy could never deceive his wife with quite the same facility that he could impress his sons, Linda serves as a kind of conscience making him confess his true earnings and his real sense of inadequacy—'The trouble is, Linda, people don't seem to take to me.' The temporary feeling of intimacy with his wife reminds Willy that he has not even been honest with Linda, and he attempts to justify his infidelity to himself —'I get so lonely—specially when business is bad. . . . I get the feeling that I'll never sell anything again, that I won't make a living for you, or . . . a business for the boys.' But even this rationalisation is undercut by the intrusion of the image of the woman in the Boston hotel room and the reminder that, in some ways, he had been more generous to his mistress than to his wife. As he approaches the final unspeakable fear—the possibility that he has betrayed Biff too by the double folly of lying and being found out—the voices become more and more accusing. Nevertheless Willy represses the memories and cries out his denial—'I never in my life told him anything but decent things.' When he returns to the present he is like a man who has glimpsed the ultimate horror, and his immediate impulse is to protect his innocence. At first he tries to blame his failure on tactics or an error in strategy—'Why didn't I go to Alaska with my brother Ben. . . . What a mistake!' But the memories pushing up into his consciousness will not let him accept that lie. The first recollection of Ben shows Willy's subconscious fear that the things he has been telling his sons were not always as decent as he had claimed—'I've been waiting for you so long! What's the answer?'

DEATH OF A SALESMAN AS A PSYCHOLOGICAL DRAMA

This subtle exploration of Willy's subjective life has led many critics to approach the play as a psychological drama with strong Freudian colouring. According to this interpretation, the work concentrates on family relationships and especially on the conflicts between fathers and sons. . . . Indeed one of the most striking characteristics of Willy is that he is both father and son. The quintessential boy-man, Willy is the eternal adolescent arrested at an early stage of development and because of it unable to help his own son to a healthy maturity. In a very real sense Willy and Biff are more like brothers than father and son, and it is Biff who grows up first.

Willy's problems as a father are shown to be a direct result of his own deprivation as a son, and it is part of the richness of *Death of a Salesman* that its perspective encompasses three generations. Willy's memories touch on the critical moments of his life and the earliest of these concern his hazy recollections of his own father—'All I remember is a man with a big beard, and I was in Mama's lap, sitting around a fire, and some kind of high music.' The music, of course, is the flute music which sounds periodically through the play and which, Miller informs us in the stage directions, tells of 'grass, trees and the horizon'. The pastoral associations of the music are related to the wanderings of the Loman family 'through Ohio, and Indiana, Michigan, Illinois, and all the Western states' where the elder Loman made and sold his flutes. But the father-image evoked by the music is much more complex than is sometimes suggested. For, according to Ben at least, their father was also a 'great inventor' who 'with one gadget' could make more in a week than Willy would make in a lifetime. The patriarch of the Loman family is therefore a shadowy ideal who embodies a variety of qualities. Musician, craftsman, salesman, inventor (as well as wife-deserter), he is a combination Wandering Jew and Yankee pedlar who has left a mingled heritage to his sons.

Since their father left when Willy was a child, he remains a dim figure in his son's imagination. Willy's determination to give strong guidance to his sons is a result of his sense of the lack of such guidance in his own life. 'Dad left when I was such a baby . . . I never had a chance to talk to him and

I still feel—kind of temporary about myself.' Willy has chosen
to imitate the salesman side of his father, not through any
urging on his father's part but rather as a result of circumstances. The most influential of these was his meeting with
David Singleman, an old New England salesman who came
to represent for Willy the father he never knew. It is Singleman's life, and more especially his death, that come to sym-
bolise what Willy thinks he wants for himself. As he explains
to Howard,

> Old Dave, he'd go up to his room, y'understand, put on his
> green velvet slippers—I'll never forget—and pick up his
> phone and call the buyers, and without even leaving his room,
> at the age of eighty-four, he made his living. And when I saw
> that, I realised that selling was the greatest career a man could
> want.

Miller almost certainly intended the irony implied by Willy's
interest in a job that required no more effort than lifting a
phone, but the more dreadful irony relates to the interpretation of business which Willy derives from Singleman's example. What Singleman's achievement represents to Willy is
a demonstration of the co-operative and benevolent nature of
capitalism. Singleman's ability to sell by phone at age eighty-
four was proof to Willy that he was 'remembered and loved
and helped by so many different people'. This conclusion
seemed to be confirmed by Singleman's funeral which was
attended by hundreds of salesmen and buyers. Singleman, in
other words, represented free enterprise with a human face,
and it is part of Willy's tragedy that he never realises that
such a system does not exist.

Willy's inability to see the nature of the system in which he
functions is the more extraordinary in that part of him wor-
ships the very ruthlessness that helps to destroy him. The
other side of his father—the inventive and irresponsible side
—is epitomised in the play by Ben who, as Willy's older
brother, constitutes another substitute father-figure. The
character of Ben differs from all the other figures in the play
in several respects. There is a quality of unreality about Ben
which suggests the generalised characters of Expressionist
drama. He refuses to answer questions about himself and
communicates cryptically—'when I walked into the jungle, I
was seventeen. When I walked out I was twenty-one. And, by
God, I was rich!' There is no attempt on Miller's part to reveal
Ben's psychological make-up, and indeed the character

MILLER'S REFLECTIONS ON HIS FATHER

In his autobiography, Timebends, *Miller reflects on the competitive relationship that he had with his father.*

I was not aware that for the rest of [my father's] life, which lasted some four more years, he spent considerable time on the lookout for his name in the gossip columns and entertainment news, until one day he gravely asked me—he was about eighty then—"Do you look like me or do I look like you?"

This was serious. "I guess I look like you," I said. He seemed to like that answer.

How strange it was—not only had I competed with him but he with me. And the fact that this vaguely disappointed me signaled that even now I saw him partly shrouded in his myth.

He was an American and saw all things competitively. Once our old basset, Hugo, an immense dog whose incontinence was matched only by his lassitude, rose like a senator from one of his naps and unaccountably attacked a rag doll, throwing it up in the air and growling menacingly at it and charging at it again and again until he settled down once more into his habitual torpor with one ear covering his eyes. My father had watched in surprise all this uncustomary activity and then said, "Well . . . everybody has to be better than somebody."

---

seems almost a two-dimensional projection of Willy's imagination. Ben is the only character who appears to Willy out of an historical context, and he seems at times to be more like a ghost or *alter ego*. It is probable that he represents in part Willy's depression over his brother's recent death and the breaking of the last connection with his father. But perhaps he functions primarily as a dramatic embodiment of those qualities of assurance, daring and lack of scruples which Willy secretly admires but does not possess. The 'jungle' where no one fights fair is where Willy knows the wealth is to be found, but his own nature yearns for the security of home, garden and an adoring family.

WILLY'S FAILURE AS A FATHER

One aspect of the play, therefore, deals with Willy Loman as a son trying to please a father he never knew. His own nature is ill-suited for the competitive world of business and he tries to adjust in two ways. He convinces himself and his sons that success is a product of being well-liked, but at the same time he encourages competitive and even unlawful behaviour. He fails because he never understands the inconsistency in his beliefs and that his desire for the emotional security of popularity is at odds with the realities of the profession he has entered.

> CHARLEY: The only thing you got in this world is what you can sell. And the funny thing is that you're a salesman, and you don't know that.
>
> WILLY: I've always tried to think otherwise, I guess.

Willy's failure to come to terms with his own father cripples him in his ability to be a father in his turn. Deprived of affection as a child, he smothers his own sons with love, and oppresses them with the nakedness of his hopes for their success. Here it is important to comprehend the paradoxical nature of the 'conflict' between Willy and his children. For what Hap, and especially Biff, have to fight is not indifference or hostility, but a surfeit of love. The terrible irony of the play is that Willy's struggles, sacrifice and final suicide are not for his own material advancement, but for his sons. Even when Biff is thirty-four years old Willy cannot rid himself of the compulsion to help him. When Charley gives him the advice of the practical realist Willy cannot take it.

> CHARLEY: He won't starve. None a them starve. Forget about him.
>
> WILLY: Then what have I got to remember?
>
> CHARLEY: You take it too hard. To hell with it. When a deposit bottle is broken you don't get your nickel back.

It is this overwhelming need to have his sons succeed that is the underlying drive of his life and the cause of his tragic agony.

Willy Loman's Illusions

Nada Zeineddine

Nada Zeineddine writes that Willy Loman's quest to find himself lacks two crucial insights: First, he fails to integrate realistically into society and second, he fails to maintain an accurate psychological sense of himself. Instead, Willy denies his authentic self by wearing a social mask that presents the image of a successful personality. Willy lives a lie. Zeineddine suggests that Willy's detachment from reality is powerfully enhanced by the expressionistic form of the play. Much of the drama takes place in Willy's head as he flits back and forth between real events and memories and disjointed thought processes. Willy's disconnected inner world is represented by the contrast between the claustrophobic urban setting and the flute sounds, which represent Willy's pipe dreams.

Zeineddine maintains that Willy's own failure as a salesman is interconnected with his failure as a father. His inability to secure a position in the business world is echoed by his inability to secure stability in his family. Biff discovers Willy to be a fake who fails to meet both his son's standards and the standards of society. Biff rejects his father, ultimately piercing through Willy's mask of false dreams.

Nada Zeineddine teaches at the University of Leicester, Great Britain.

In *Death of a Salesman* Miller further explores the implications of the impact of the system on the breadwinner, his fears of being thrown out of the system, of ceasing to be because he ceases to have. Willy Loman does not commit a crime, thus he is less of a misfit in human terms, but he is a breadwinner and, as such, he must have standardized responses to the system, to be, in W.H. Auden's[1] words, 'an ideal citizen'.

1. English poet and dramatist

WILLY'S QUEST FOR SELF

Death of a Salesman grapples with the problems caused by the individual's maladjustment to social demands, and his failure to achieve the minimal degree of integration between individual and collective concerns. Like *All My Sons, Death of a Salesman* sets the struggle within society against the background of the family. While *All My Sons* places primary emphasis on the social and universal implications of Joe Keller's transgression against specific ethical codes of conduct, the later play delineates the psychological implications of Willy Loman's transgression against social codes of conduct.

Willy Loman embarks on a quest for his self. He fails, however, to recognize the fact that finding one's self involves not only social integration but also accurate psychological insight. *Death of a Salesman* focuses on the tragic consequences of social conformity, and the fatal results of inauthenticity. Willy shares basic affinities with Mrs Alving.[2] Like her, he fails to coin the metal in himself, and subsequently renounces his real authentic being in favour of a mask. Mrs Alving had donned the mask of a dutiful housewife; Willy Loman wears that of a 'number one' man. To Mrs Alving and Willy, masks are the only means of maintaining an identity in the social masquerade, and of eliminating their fear of separateness. Masks may be identified with identity. Like Mrs Alving, Willy's life is built on a lie. In fact, the idea of a life-lie that features prominently in *Ghosts* and *Pillars of Society* and lies at the very core of *The Wild Duck* is vividly dramatized by Miller. Life is a 'pipedream'—to borrow O'Neill's condensation of the expression—and a 'pipedream' renders life more endurable.

Willy Loman appears on the scene performing his final staggering steps in life—a life of continual stumbling mistaken by him for a glide on the smooth road of success.

EXPRESSIONISTIC FORM OF *DEATH OF A SALESMAN*

The method of the play is suggested in the subtitle 'Certain Private Conversations in Two Acts and a Requiem'. These private conversations, with resonances of Strindberg's[3] intimate theatre, are held between Willy and himself, and Willy and the audience. For a considerable part of the play the stage is set in Willy's head where the past finds its way into

2. Character in Ibsen's *Ghosts* 3. Swedish playwright, August

the present of this decaying dreamer. Arthur Miller holds that the original title of the play was *The Inside of His Head,* and that the nucleus of the play's creation resided in an image 'of an enormous face the height of the proscenium arch which would appear and then open up, and we would see the inside of a man's head'. In contrast to the Ibsenesque retrospective structure employed in *All My Sons, Death of a Salesman* evolves its meaning through the gradual unfolding of simultaneously existing experiences in Willy's 'head'. Miller contends that:

> The *Salesman* image was from the beginning absorbed with the concept that nothing in life comes 'next' but that everything exists together and at the same time within us; that there is no past to be 'brought forward' in a human being, but that he is his past at every moment and that the present is merely that which his past is capable of noticing and smelling and reacting to.

The 'inside' of Willy's head is indeed the stage of many incidents demonstrating his severance from any connections of compromising stances with reality.

Miller attempts to relate his expressionistic method to Willy's psychology. The playwright manages to achieve a high degree of integration between his form and content, but that integration in itself makes it increasingly difficult to define the interpreter's stance. As the temporal framework of the play fluctuates and as Willy's awareness of his problem varies from scene to scene, the analysis of the play invites an intrusion on the part of the interpreter which would at best attempt to take account of Miller's integration of form and content. The interpreter's attempt to articulate experiences that leave Willy either literally or metaphorically inarticulate necessitates very often an act of reading into Willy's actions.

THE MEANING OF THE PLAY'S PHYSICAL SETTING

Miller delineates Willy's inner world, both musically and scenically, through his description of the physical setting. The setting of *Death of a Salesman* is described as such:

> *A melody is heard, played upon a flute. It is small and fine, telling of grass and trees and the horizon. The curtain rises.*
>
> *Before us is the SALESMAN'S house. We are aware of towering, angular shapes behind it, surrounding it on all sides. Only the blue light of the sky falls upon the house and forestage; the surrounding area shows an angry glow of orange. As more light appears, we see a solid vault of apartment*

houses around the small, fragile-seeming home. An air of the
dream clings to the place, a dream rising out of reality.

These stage directions suggest the contrast drawn in the play
between the actual world with its claustrophobic depressing
buildings which are symptomatic of the commercial and artificial world, and the elemental dream world of the flute. It
is for this bygone world of simple tunes escaping from the
flute that Willy yearns—a world not yet corrupted by ma-
chine-produced sounds. Willy's dilemma stems partially
from his failure to acknowledge his estrangement from the
urban culture to which he has committed himself. Miller articulates Willy's mental excursions by impregnating words,
objects, and gestures with meaning. Willy's persistence in
inhabiting a world of dreams makes him lack focus on reality. This predicament is suggested in his words to Linda:

> I was driving along, you understand? And I was fine. I was
> even observing the scenery. You can imagine, me looking at
> scenery, on the road every week of my life. But it's so beauti-
> ful up there, Linda, the trees are so thick, and the sun is
> warm. I opened the windshield and just let the warm air
> bathe over me. And then all of a sudden I'm goin' off the road!
> I'm tellin' ya, I absolutely forgot I was driving. If I'd've gone
> the other way over the white line I might've killed somebody.
> So I went on again—and five minutes later I'm dreamin'
> again, and I nearly—[*He presses two fingers against his eyes.*]
> I have such thoughts, I have such strange thoughts.

Willy presses his eyes. They are sore because of what they
can see or perhaps not see. To evade the sterile present Willy
constantly lives in the past:

> The street is lined with cars. There's not a breath of fresh air
> in the neighbourhood. The grass don't grow any more, you
> can't raise a carrot in the back yard. They should've had a law
> against apartment houses. Remember those two beautiful
> elm trees out there.

The open spaces and natural expanses Willy yearns for contrast with the stifling effect of a social context. This point
about Willy brings to mind a useful comparison with Oswald.[4] Willy is, in a way, restating the dichotomy Oswald
Alving draws between home and abroad. In Willy's case, it is
home divided within itself: home as it was and home as it is.
The claustrophobic fear of being stifled by the present, en-
gendered in Oswald, similarly torments Willy. Both Oswald
and Willy seek creativity; yet both are doomed to impotence.

4. Character in Ibsen's *Ghosts*

Willy is a talented craftsman. Miller holds that the nature of salesmanship requires 'ingenuity and individualism', and adds that a salesman is a creative person because he has to 'conceive a plan of attack and use kinds of ingenuity'. It is, however, clearly the creativity stemming from the use of his own hands that Willy possesses.

WILLY'S SPLINTERED FAMILY

Willy's great dreams of success do not only centre on himself, but they also embrace his sons, Biff and Happy. A stickler for the 'cult of personality', he pours the following advice into their ears: 'Be liked and you will never want.'

Death of a Salesman dramatizes the decay of a man forced to witness his own social failure, the deflation of his dreams, and the disintegration of his own family. The title embodies the social aspect of Willy's failure. However, the play is as much concerned with the death of a father as with that of a salesman. Any interpretation of the play must take into consideration the fact that Willy's shortcomings as a salesman and as a father are inextricably linked. Willy's search for a secure position within the family is inseparable from his search for a definite one in the 'success' system. On both fronts he fails drastically.

Willy Loman confesses to being 'temporary' about himself. To take the stance of the capitalistic society in which Willy is responsible to a productive pattern, Willy is alienated by society. He does not fit into a pattern of efficiency. Miller highlights the loneliness Willy suffers in the course of his search for identity. The disorientation of Willy's relations with the wider society is reflected in a confusion and imbalance within his family, and in his own estrangement from it. Basic to the play is the situation where the father is separated from his sons and the mother from sons and father, in an attempt to reconcile them.

The causes of the splintered familial relations are revealed in the course of the play as lying in the rather private act of Willy's infidelity. Destructive in its effect, it creates a friction between father and son, which is incomprehensible to Linda and Happy. Biff's discovery of his 'hero' in a Boston hotel with a mistress has a shattering effect on him. Consequently, Biff refuses to go to college and leads a reckless existence. Biff views his father's act as unpardonable. Like Chris Keller, Biff Loman is disillusioned with his father. 'You

fake! You phony little fake! You fake!' is by no means a condemnation any father would like to hear, particularly when
he knows it is well deserved. Willy is a 'fake' in two interrelated ways. He fails to live up to Biff's set standards of a
father by committing himself to a false set of social values.
Throughout his life Willy is unaware of the fact that what he
really craves is simple fulfilment as a father. His warped vision has confused his ideals of fatherhood with the idea of
success in a social sphere.

BIFF'S CONFRONTATION WITH WILLY

By observing his father's mode of life, Biff gradually realizes
that he cannot tolerate living in a materialistic society. He
tries to break through Willy's maze of dreams, and force
upon Willy the realization of his own limitations. Once more
father and son face each other, thus recalling similar confrontations between Joe and Chris Keller, and anticipating
the conflict between Williams's[5] Big Daddy and Brick in *Cat
on a Hot Tin Roof.* Biff explains that he is not the great son
of Willy's dreams, and that his failure is grafted in Willy's
failure as a father. He resentfully refers to the destructive effect of his knowledge of Willy's adultery:

> You know why I had no address for three months? I stole a
> suit in Kansas City and I was in jail.

Biff becomes aware of his position in society. He does not
want to be, like his father, a man in the wrong place at the
wrong time. Referring to an unsuccessful business interview, Biff voices his rejection of business life and his desire
to be what he 'is' and not what he 'should' be:

> And in the middle of that office building, do you hear this? I
> stopped in the middle of that building and I saw—the sky. I
> saw the things that I love in this world. The work and the food
> and the time to sit and smoke. . . . Why am I trying to become
> what I don't want to be? What am I doing in an office, mak-
> ing a contemptuous, begging fool of myself, when all I want
> is out there, waiting for me the minute I say I know who I am!

Unfortunately, Willy has no answer for Biff's probing questions. If he had but the semblance of an answer he would not
have become a 'fake' and a failure. Throughout his life Willy
has compensated for his social failure by dreams of personal
success and popularity. In fact, Biff makes the most accurate
judgement of his father's flaw and pinpoints the source of

5. American playwright, Tennessee

his dilemma in the words 'He [Willy] had the wrong dream'. Willy is misled by the great American dream. Underlying this view of life is the false assumption that the secret of success lies in being 'well-liked'. His inability to perceive the multi-facetedness of social demands accounts largely for his problem. Willy Loman, in fact, embodies the absurdity and triviality of a society that places faith in appearances. Willy could have been a good craftsman, but he misguidedly pursued that kind of success which would bring him social recognition and 'comradeship'. The moment of illumination is now over for Biff; he pierces further through his father's gauze of dreams:

> I am not a leader of men, Willy, and neither are you. You were never anything but a hard-working drummer who landed in the ash can like all the rest of them! I'm one dollar an hour, Willy! I tried seven states and couldn't raise it. A buck an hour! Do you gather my meaning? I'm not bringing home any prizes any more, and you're going to stop waiting for me to bring them home.

Finally, Biff breaks down after this highly charged scene and sobs in Willy's arms. Movingly, he pleads:

> Will you take that phony dream and burn it before something happens?

Willy realizes that Biff loves him after all. This knowledge overwhelms him and exacerbates his feeling of guilt for not deserving this love. His main concern centres subsequently on finding a way to rewardingly reciprocate this undeserved love. At one point, when the past is being merged with the present, Willy pathetically expresses his elation at this discovery of Biff's love to his brother Ben:

> Oh, Ben, I always knew one way or another we were gonna make it, Biff and I!

Ben functions as a bridge connecting Willy with the bygone world of the flute. Willy's conversations with Ben heighten the former's failure both as son and brother. It is Ben who had ventured independently into the world. Ben is a living reminder to Willy of what he might have been. Ben has discovered his own resources and advantageously worked on them.

Having been confronted with a revelation of his son's love, Willy meanders down the paths of his mind to discuss with Ben a proposition of his own suicide. Willy maintains his false ideals to the very end. By committing suicide he will raise twenty thousand dollars for his beloved 'Adonis'. He thus intends to pay for Biff's love. Moreover, Willy probably regards the idea of suicide as a kind of atonement for, and relief from, the intolerable guilt he feels for his failure as a salesman and a father. Willy had always viewed his children as his future life. Miller states that one of the images the play grew from was 'the image of a need greater than hunger or sex or thirst, a need to leave a thumbprint somewhere on the world. A need for immortality, and by admitting it, the knowing that one has carefully inscribed one's name on a cake of ice on a hot July day.' Willy's 'future' life was annihilated since his infidelity had been discovered. From that moment he had tried to arouse his family's pity and attention by contemplating unsuccessful suicidal acts.

Willy Loman dies a lonely man. His is not the death of his ideal salesman Dave Singleman. It is rather the death of a 'single' man alienated from self, family and society, and accompanied only by burdens of guilt and needs of atonement. The only exit Willy can see is suicide.

A Comparison of Ronald Reagan and Willy Loman

John S. Shockley

John S. Shockley asserts that *Death of a Salesman* remains a powerful play that resonates in American life and culture. To support this claim, Shockley draws similarities between Willy Loman and a dominate figure of the late twentieth century, Ronald Reagan. Shockley outlines many parallel character traits between the two. Both denied aspects of reality to believe in the American dream: Willy denied his personal and family failures while Ronald Reagan often lacked interest in facts or misstated them to fit his personal agenda. Both fantasized to bolster their confidence and to avoid unpleasant realities: Willy fantasized about his role as a salesman and Reagan played off his movie image as the Gipper, Notre Dame's football hero. Shockley writes that both figures were unable to form close personal relationships and both, suffering from family problems, relied on their wives to protect and bolster them. Moreover, both Loman and Reagan overlooked the ugly side of the American creed of success.

Shockley concludes that Miller presages the Reagan prototype. Miller understood the American need for meaning, even if it requires selective perception, denial, and fantasy. Reagan, America's super salesman, understood the efficacy of hyping American optimism in order to sell the American dream.

John Shockley teaches courses in politics and drama at Gustavus Adolphus College, St. Peter, Minnesota.

Death of a Salesman hit the American stage in 1949, catapulting Arthur Miller into the status of the "greats" of American dramatists. While the play was never without its critics, who argued over whether the play could appropriately be called a "tragedy,"

Excerpted from John Shockley, "*Death of a Salesman* and American Leadership: Life Imitates Art," *Journal of American Culture*, vol. 17, no. 2 (Summer 1994), pp. 49–56. Reprinted by permission of the publisher. Endnotes in the original have been omitted here.

whether the writing was a bit stilted, and whether Miller's message about American capitalism and the American dream was a bit garbled, it still was an enormously popular play among theater-goers and critics. All of them seemed to find something of the American creed, and of themselves, in the play.

But more than 40 years have passed since the play was written. Should we now view the play as a dated relic of another age, or does it still resonate with the American character? Is the play primarily the personal problem of an aging playwright whose formative years were spent in the Great Depression, and who therefore could never "trust" American capitalism again? If so, do we have little need to understand *Death of a Salesman* or come to terms with it? On the contrary, I shall argue that *Death of a Salesman* still resonates powerfully in American life and culture and that in a fascinating and chilling way life has imitated drama. Willy Loman shares a number of important traits with the most successful American politician of the late twentieth century, Ronald Reagan. To understand American culture and American politics, one must come to grips with the phenomenal success of Ronald Reagan. Arthur Miller's perspective in creating Willy Loman and *Death of a Salesman* can help us do this.

RONALD REAGAN AND WILLY LOMAN AS SALESMEN

The Similarities of Willy Loman and Ronald Reagan   In the first place, both Willy Loman and Ronald Reagan are salesmen. Both understood that a salesman has got to believe in himself and his product before he can sell it to others. Both were selling themselves and the American dream. Ronald Reagan, of course, was a salesman for General Electric, "living well electrically" while touting the corporation's conservative political agenda. But most of all, as he gave "The Speech" to 250,000 GE employees while traveling all over the country, he sold the American dream. And he was selling that both before and after his years as a GE salesman.

After he was dropped by GE, he became a salesman for the conservative ideas of Southern California businessmen, who recognized in him the best spokesman for their ideology that they could find. "A salesman has got to dream, boy. It comes with the territory." So says Charlie, Willy's neighbor, at Willy's funeral. Both Willy and Reagan dreamed the American dream and believed that in America a man could, and should, fulfill himself.

A SHARED SENSE OF DENIAL

Second, both also had to deny basic points of reality in order to believe in the dream. Willy tried desperately to deny that his sons were failures and that he was failing as a salesman. His son Biff is always about to be a success, about to land a good job. And Willy lies to Linda about the source of his income, telling her the money is coming from sales when in fact Charlie down the street is lending him the money. Throughout the play he is always lying about how important he is and how many "friends" he has. Ronald Reagan, as the son of a failed, alcoholic, shoe salesman, was forced to deny his family's problems from an early age. Ronald Reagan is the adult child of an alcoholic. Yet his father's skills as a raconteur and his mother's encouragement of his acting and entertaining abilities channeled the denials and "stories" into more acceptable outlets than Willy had. As Willy loved telling jokes to highlight his personality, Reagan loved entertaining others. Denials continued throughout Reagan's life: denying that Hollywood had engaged in a blacklist; denying that the MCA (Music Corporation of America) was involved in bribery and "payola" while Reagan dealt with them as president of the Screen Actors Guild; denying that his tax cuts could be responsible for the mounting federal deficits; denying that his cuts in low-income housing subsidies could be responsible for the rise in homelessness; denying that he sold arms for hostages; and forgetting virtually everything about the Iran-Contra diversion scandal.

To scholars of the Reagan era, one of the most striking features of Reagan the man was his lack of interest in facts, which were often misstated or completely wrong. His view of "facts" was entirely utilitarian, in service to his ideology of the American dream and American foreign policy. Willy too had great difficulty absorbing facts that did not fit the view he wanted to have of himself and his life. The entire play is basically a struggle within Willy's mind between his vision of himself and the painful reality of facts intruding upon his "dream." Perhaps the most painful and poignant moment in the play comes when his son Biff tries to tell Willy that he's not now and will never be the "success" Willy imagines for him. Willy cannot hear him. Actually, in denying basic facts each man was trying to create himself from myth. One was of course more successful at doing this than the other.

A SHARED DENIAL OF REALITY

Third, Ronald Reagan and Willy Loman also had to fantasize in order to avoid the realities they could not handle and to give themselves the confidence they otherwise would lack. Willy was "well liked" and known all over New England, and at his own funeral his boys would be impressed at how many "friends" would show up. Ronald Reagan moved more than a dozen times during his childhood, and had to learn to survive without close friends. He wanted to play football but was never any good (his eyes were too poor). Yet he was "the Gipper," Notre Dame's great football hero, throughout his political career. His movie career and political career often blended, sometimes consciously as in the above example, and sometimes unconsciously. The "Gipper" was a kind of double fantasy, in that George Gipp himself was a mythical hero based heavily on fantasy. While "Win One For the Gipper," Reagan's favorite movie and political line, probably was said by George Gipp on his death bed, most likely Gipp thought he was talking to his doctor. In reality, George Gipp was a rather unsavory character who bet on his own games and by today's standards would have been expelled from the sport. But, as with so much of Ronald Reagan and Willy Loman, facts were not allowed to get in the way of the myth. And in another kind of chilling rehearsal for life (politics) imitating art (the movie), the Reagan movie helped make Gipp into "a teflon hero."

A SHARED NEED TO BE WELL LIKED

Fourth, while both Willy and Reagan wanted to be well liked, and wanted to have the personalities to "win friends and influence people," neither was successful at forming close personal friendships. In both cases, only their wives stood by them, and in both cases their wives tried to protect them and sustain their husbands' illusions in the face of reality. Each man tried to make sure his "image" presented an air of leadership and success, but both men in fact were more passive than they wanted to appear.

Both men also faced severe problems with their children and denied these problems to themselves and the outside world. Willy's pained relationships with his two sons is one of the basic themes running through *Death of a Salesman.* With Reagan, his relationship with his adopted son Michael (detailed in Michael's autobiography, *On the Outside Looking In*) has been extremely strained. His daughter Patti barely has been on speaking terms with her parents since the publication of her autobiography (thinly disguised as a novel) several years ago (*Home Front*). Both men lacked strong fathers who could nurture them, although their father relationships also contained important differences. In a poignant moment, Willy asks Ben (his older brother) to tell him more about "Dad," who left when Willy was still young, because "I still feel kind of temporary about myself." Reagan had a much longer relationship with his father, but Reagan's stay in any one place was "kind of temporary." Jack Reagan was also "footloose." He moved constantly, changed jobs, and was usually a failure as a salesman. In addition, Reagan's father's alcoholism was a source of worry and shame. But Ronald Reagan also described his father as "the best raconteur I ever heard," and this surely must have helped Ronald's own skills as a salesman and storyteller.

Fifth, both men had brushes with the uglier side of capitalism, and yet seemed unable to recognize or condemn this brutal side. To Willy it was his older brother Ben, who became a millionaire at a young age and kept admonishing Willy: "Never fight fair with a stranger, boy. You'll never get out of the jungle that way." Yet Willy constantly wants Ben's approval and is asking him how he managed to be so successful. Willy even views his son Biff's stealing as "initiative."

Reagan was called before a grand jury investigating the seamier side of Hollywood capitalism, the bribery and monopolistic practices of the Music Corporation of America. Its special sweet deals with the Screen Actors Guild while Reagan was president of the Guild and simultaneously getting what looked like kickbacks from MCA nearly resulted in his indictment.

Later, as President, Reagan was surrounded by corruption, influence peddling, indictments, trials and convictions of his aides and associates—Michael Deaver, Lynn Nofziger, John Poindexter—the HUD scandal, the Savings and Loan scandal and the spectacular corruption of some who became multimillionaires during his era. But throughout his administration and throughout *Death of a Salesman* neither Reagan nor Willy ever criticized or condemned any actions by these people. As Willy refused to condemn son Biff's stealing or brother Ben's ruthlessness, neither did Reagan condemn the stealings and illegalities of any of his aides. Neither had a moral code of what were fair and unfair practices, what were proper ways to get rich and what were improper ways. To both, the American creed meant success and riches, but *how* these were obtained neither wanted to examine too closely. Perhaps they did not want to examine this too closely because the truth would have been too painful. To both men America and the American creed seemed to have no place for failure. How one succeeded was therefore not a moral question.

Both the Reagan presidency and *Death of a Salesman* then are dramas about the power of the American dream and the self-deceptions necessary for the kind of American dream believed. These are both potent forces in American politics and culture. . . .

Arthur Miller, through Willy Loman, presages the Reagan prototype through 1) emphasizing the power of the capitalist-consumerist-get-rich-and-be-well-liked dream, and the hold it has on the American people. Miller shows us the power of the myth. 2) He also understood the need for selective perception, fantasy and denial, and the tenuous hold on reality necessary for this strident view of the dream. He prepares us for the Reagan denials, misstatements and lies, and the gap between appearance and reality. To both Willy and Reagan, uttering the cliches of success is virtually the same thing as bringing these cliches into actuality. To both, "saying makes it so," and thus they are an evasion of the truth. Arthur Miller helps us understand that Ronald Reagan succeeded not in spite of but because of all his paradoxes and contradictions. As the defender of the little man's dream, he succeeded because millionaires could use him to champion a dream that benefitted primarily themselves. If he had been truly committed to helping the little Willys of the nation fulfill their dreams, he would have been dumped by his financial backers. . . .

Miller also seems to understand that 3) as pressures on the dream close in, the desire to believe in it will intensify rather than weaken. The American people did not want to hear Jimmy Carter (or John Anderson or Walter Mondale or Bruce Babbitt, etc.) any more than Willy wanted to hear Charlie. A "realist," willing to talk of limits, taxes, sacrifice and mixed motives in a complex world isn't what Willy or the American people wanted to hear. Arthur Miller understood this form of the American psyche and its power.

Surely all writers—political analysts as well as dramatists—recognize the need of people to find meaning in their lives. But Miller understood the particular nature of the American need for meaning. Through giving us Willy Loman, Miller helped us better understand the successful Willy Loman when he appeared on the American stage: Ronald Reagan, the super salesman, everything Willy and our nation of Willys wanted to be. Ronald Reagan understood American fears, hopes, lies, vulnerabilities and the need for optimism better than many political scientists, and he understood the role of the salesman in selling us our dreams better than others did. He had the confidence the rest of us wanted.

But whether we should assess Reagan as critically as son Biff assessed Willy—"He had the wrong dreams. All, all wrong"—is less clear. After a decade of Reagan and Reaganism we have record budget deficits, record trade deficits, increased dependence upon foreign lenders in the world economy, a crumbling infrastructure and, most poignant and ironic of all, a growing gap between rich and poor. It is now harder, not easier, for the little Willys of society to reach the American dream. To criticize Reagan, we, like Biff, would have to condemn part of ourselves, condemn part of our own dreams, and condemn part of our identity and meaning as Americans. We Americans are a long way from being ready or able to do that. But we should not forget that both Willy Loman and Ronald Reagan embody what ought to be a debate about the essence and direction of America.

Willy Loman and the American Dream

Thomas E. Porter

Thomas Porter discusses Willy Loman as a representative of an American salesman of the lower middle class who has been shaped by forces in the culture. Willy's social status, his family background, and his role as a salesman stem from the conditioning of an American producer-consumer-driven society. Willy's type is uniquely American in origin and rooted in the success myth of the rags-to-riches romance of the American dream. Porter explains that the play attacks this myth by portraying not only Willy's failure, but the failure of the success dream itself. For Willy and those he represents, the dream never materializes. Porter writes that Miller, utilizing a flexible expressionistic setting, successfully contrasts the dream world of Willy and the modest world in which the Lomans live.

Thomas E. Porter is a professor of English at the University of Texas at Arlington. He teaches modern drama and is the Dean of Liberal Arts.

The most salient quality of Arthur Miller's tragedy of the common man *Death of a Salesman* is its Americanism. This quality in the play is demonstrated by the contrasting reactions of American and English reviewers. The English took the hero at face value and found little of interest in his person or his plight:

> There is almost nothing to be said for Loman who lies to himself as to others, has no creed or philosophy of life beyond that of making money by making buddies, and cannot even be faithful to his helpful and long-suffering wife.

Brooks Atkinson, on the other hand, thought Willy "a good man who represents the homely, decent, kindly virtues of a middle-class society." The Englishman treats Willy without regard for his American context, the New York reviewer sees

Reprinted from *Myth and Modern American Drama*, by Thomas E. Porter, by permission of the Wayne State University Press. Copyright © 1969 by Wayne State University Press.

him as the representative of a large segment of American society. When the literary critics measure the play against
Greek and Elizabethan drama, they agree with the English
evaluation; the hero seems inadequate. His lack of stature,
his narrow view of reality, his obvious character defects di-
minish the scope of the action and the possibilities of universal applications. Against a large historical perspective and
without the American context, the salesman is a "small man"
who fails to cope with his environment. But for better or
worse, Miller's hero is not simply an individual who has determined on an objective and who strives desperately to attain it; he is also representative of an American type, the
Salesman, who has accepted an ideal shaped for him and
pressed on him by forces in his culture. This ideal is the ma-
trix from which Willy emerges and by which his destiny is
determined. It is peculiarly American in origin and development—seed, flower and fruit. For Arthur Miller's salesman is
a personification of the success myth; he is committed to its
objectives and defined by its characteristics. *Salesman* deals
with the Horatio Alger[1] ideal, the rags-to-riches romance of
the American dream. . . .

DEATH OF A SALESMAN AS ANTI-MYTH

The success myth, in the hands of the playwright, becomes
the model for the events of the plot, the situation and the
character of the hero, but Miller uses this model in order to
subvert it. His play is an anti-myth, the rags-to-riches formula in reverse so that it becomes the story of a failure in
terms of success, or better, the story of the failure of the success myth. The events of the play are a mirror-image of the
hero's progress. Willy Loman's history begins at the end of
the line; instead of the young, determined bootblack an exhausted salesman enters, carrying, along with his sample
cases, sixty years of uphill struggle. The subsequent events
show him failing to overcome each obstacle, just as he has
failed to achieve the phantom success he has pursued his life
long. He returns from a trip without making a single sale, he
braces the boss for a New York job and a salary raise (like the
Alger hero) and is fired for his pains; his "boys," now well out
of boyhood, make the big play for high stakes according to
their father's teaching and fail. Willy finishes by facing the

1. American writer of books for boys

harsh fact that his whole life has been a lie. The triumphal ascent of the Alger hero is reversed in every particular. The rags-to-riches dream never materializes, and the salesman never escapes his rags. The race with the junkyard finds Willy an also-ran. In the collapse of the salesman, Miller attempts to illustrate the collapse of the myth.

Death of a Salesman encompasses two dimensions—the dreamworld of the success myth with its merging of past triumphs, indications of glory to come, glimmering possibilities and the actual world of the small, brick-enclosed house in Brooklyn. To achieve this merger, Miller uses an expressionistic setting, a skeletonized house which symbolizes the encroachment of urban economics on the family. The "one-dimensional" roof is surrounded on all sides by a "solid vault of apartment houses." The walls of the Loman home are cut away to permit free passage to the personae in dream and reminiscence sequences. This device, along with changes in lighting, allows for a condensation of time so that the life of the family can be encompassed by the action. "An air of the dream clings to the place, a dream rising out of reality." The expressionistic technique—the use of typical personae, a symbolic setting, mobility in time—follows on the mythic focus of the playwright's vision. Miller himself is conscious of the possibilities of this technique and its significance; he defines expressionism: "The stage is stripped of knickknacks; instead it reveals symbolic *designs* which function as overt pointers toward the moral to be drawn from the action." The freedom which this technique supplies allows the playwright to express the salesman's dream and his experiences in the context of the dream. The flashbacks in the course of the action can be considered hallucinatory, and the salesman can be played as mentally unbalanced, but such an interpretation takes actuality as the norm and loses sight of the mythical dimension. Any attempt to decide which elements of the play are "real" and which "unreal" is as futile as trying to sort out the "historical" elements in any myth. The mythical attitude and Willy's experiences form one texture; they are the warp and woof of the salesman's world.

THE WILLY LOMAN PERSONA

The typical characteristics of the Willy Loman persona establish him in the tradition of the mythical hero, or in S*alesman*, in the tradition of the anti-hero. The name is descriptive; Willy is "low man" on the economic and social totem-pole. Linda, his wife, who sees him clearly and sympathetically, calls him "a small man." He is a white-collar worker who works on salary and/or commission for a company, his economic future at the mercy of his employer. He does not show any marked intellectual capacity or training, and his wisdom, expressed in platitudes, is garnered from common-sense authorities. When he is away from home, his moral life functions according to the "traveling salesman" tradition, not excluding the clandestine affair or the blue joke. He does not, however, consider himself dissolute; according to his lights, he is honest enough. For better or worse, the salesman is intended to represent the average lower-middle-class American.

The antecedents of the salesman are also typical. For a man who resides in Brooklyn, the family background which Miller gives his hero stretches the imagination. In a sequence with Ben, Willy remembers his father, a man with a big beard who played the flute. His father, too, was a traveling salesman:

> BEN: Father was a very great and very wild-hearted man. We would start in Boston, and he'd toss the whole family into the wagon and then he'd drive the team right across the country; through Ohio and Indiana, Michigan, Illinois and all the Western states. And we'd stop in the towns and sell the flutes that he'd made on the way. Great inventor, Father. With one gadget he made more than a man like you could make in a lifetime.

The father disappeared one day when Willy was a baby, following the Yukon gold-strike. He lived many years in Alaska, and Willy had a yearning to join him there. This is the stock from which Willy and his boys are sprung, American stock with a penchant for traveling and selling. This background fits an idealized model rather than any plausible or realistic family-tree. As typical character, the salesman has a typical background; he envisions his origin in terms of the American experience. It is one version of the idealized experience of the race.

Willy's status in society, his family background are typical; even more of a type is Willy's identity as Salesman. He is a product of a producer-consumer society in which the go-between is a pivotal figure. Society has labeled him, and Willy has accepted the label; society has offered Willy a set of values and an objective, and Willy has committed himself to those values and that objective. In so accepting, Willy becomes THE Salesman. He cannot define himself in any other terms. So he insists in his debate with Charley that "he has a job," that he is the "New England man," even after he has been fired. His adherence to the cult of personality, of being "well liked," is a reflection of his identity; before he can sell anything and if he can sell nothing else, he must sell himself, his own personality. He has been shaped by a society that believed steadily and optimistically in the myth of success, and he has become the agent and the representative of that society.

BEN AND THE IDEALIZED PAST

This image of the Salesman includes the image of an older, freer America. Before the frontier closed down and the apartments closed in, before business became an impersonal, corporate endeavor, opportunity knocked incessantly. For Willy (and for the audience), the achievement possible in this earlier society is typified by Uncle Ben, the shadowy figure who appears out of nowhere, to the accompaniment of flute music, on his way to new capitalistic triumphs. Whether Ben is a projection of Willy's imagination or a real figure out of the family history is irrelevant; his function in the action does not depend on his "reality." He comes from an idealized past; he is the robber baron, the captain of industry. Ben carries with him the aura of success, and when he visits, it is only for a few minutes between expeditions. There are diamond mines in Africa, timberlands in Alaska, and mysterious appointments in Ketchikan which demand his attention. Ben's methods are illustrated in a sparring match with Biff. He is physically strong—Biff can hit him in the stomach with impunity. He is ruthless—the sparring ends abruptly when Ben suddenly trips the boy and poises the point of his umbrella over Biff's eye. "Never fight fair with a stranger, boy. You'll never get out of the jungle that way." This is the code of the self-made man.

Ben possesses the precious secret to success. It is summarized in his ritual chant, the formula which sums up his accomplishment: "When I was seventeen I walked into the jungle, and when I was twenty-one I walked out. And by God I was rich." What happened in the jungle is never explained. It is the mystery of success, the Eleusinian rite known only to initiates. Uncle Ben is the older version of the Salesman, the ruthless capitalist whose adventurous strength ripped riches from the frontier. To Willy, Uncle Ben is the palpable proof of his doctrine.

While the shadowy figure of Ben establishes the general truth that any man can succeed, Willy does not accept (or perhaps has no chance to accept) Ben's method. Ben represents the robber baron who travels out to unknown frontiers and ruthlessly carves out an empire. As Ben's method has faded with the passing of the empire builders and with the advent of the big corporations, Willy decides to rely on personality:

> It's not what you do, Ben. It's who you know and the smile on your face! It's contacts, Ben, contacts! The whole wealth of Alaska passes over the lunch table at the Commodore Hotel, and that's the wonder, the wonder of this country, that a man can end with diamonds here on the basis of being well liked.

This quality cannot be held in the hand like Ben's timber, but on the other hand, Ben's own formula—his inner strength and ruthlessness—is also mysterious. Willy accepts the Dale Carnegie approach to success; winning friends and influencing people become his pick and shovel to dig diamonds as industriously as Ben ever did. But Willy does not go off to Africa or Alaska, nor is his confidence in a transcendentally virtuous life. His faith in personality conceals the secret in an imponderable and makes that faith untestable by any pragmatic standard. The dream of success, in the eyes of the playwright, is the more destructive because, though indemonstrable, it has a myth-like capacity for inspiring a transcendent belief.

THE LOMAN SUCCESS IDEOLOGY

There are, however, certain tangible signs which characterize the personality likely to succeed. Willy discovers them in his sons. The boys are physically strong, well-built, attractive. Biff is a football hero, the captain of the high school team; Happy, if not gifted with Biff's athletic ability, has a pleasant personality and basks in Biff's reflected glory. Against this picture of the glowing athlete and the hail fellow, Bernard, the neighbor's boy, wears glasses, studies hard, and is not well liked. If physical prowess and a moderate anti-intellectualism seemed to have little to do with success, the propagators of the success ideology saw an intimate connection:

> Statistics show that executives are physically stronger and larger of stature than their subordinates. For example, college presidents, as a class, are taller and heavier than the college professors. Bank presidents are physically stronger than the clerks. Railway presidents are larger and physically stronger than the employees. . . . Physical welfare is the second qualification for winning the race of making good.

Biff does not have to work hard at his studies; books are not necessary for advancement. Bernard, whose scholastic efforts are the object of mild derision, supplies Biff with answers and this is only right, the homage due the personable and popular. When, in spite of Bernard's help, Biff fails in math, Willy blames the teacher. Willy shows a typical ambivalence toward education. On the one hand, attendance at college confers prestige, especially when coupled with an athletic career; on the other, education does not really make an appreciable difference in the struggle to succeed. Some self-help advocates maintained that college was actually harmful to a young man's chances. It undermined those rugged personal qualities demanded by a career by an overemphasis on the development of the mind, it fostered an interest in impractical humanistic matters, it devoured the best years of a man's life. The salesman finds in his sons those qualities which point toward success. As high-school boys, they are leaders, popular with the crowd, athletic and handsome. Their present status as philandering clerk and wandering farmhand cannot erase the glory of their past potential as Willy experienced it. "A star like that, magnificent, can never really fade away."

Willy's commitment to the success ideology directed the education of his sons. Even if success passes him by, he can still look forward to a vindication of his life in them. They have been instructed in the clichés of both the "virtue" and the "personality" school. Industry is important: whatever else can be said about Biff, he is a "hard worker." One of Willy's fondest reminiscences is the high sheen the boys kept on the red Chevy. If Biff "gets tired" hanging around, he can paint the new ceiling in the living room. Willy's aphorisms emphasize the importance of industry and perseverance: "Never leave a job till you're finished." "The world is an oyster, but you don't crack it open on a mattress." But personality has its privileges and Willy can wink at the boys' faults in the name of personality. Biff has been a thief from his high-school days; he steals a football from the locker-room and lumber from a local construction job. Willy laughs at both thefts because they reveal the power of personality and a fearless competitiveness like Ben's. "Coach will probably congratulate you on your initiative. . . . That's because he likes you. If somebody else took the ball there'd be an uproar." When Charley warns Willy that the watchman will catch the boys at their thieving,

Willy avers that, though he gave them hell, the boys are "a couple of fearless characters." When Charley responds that the jails are full of fearless characters, Ben adds that the Stock Exchange is also. The boys have been brought up to respect the success ideology; their success will be the salesman's vindication.

WILLY'S LIFE AS A LIE

In the chronological present of the play Willy's fortunes are at low ebb. His faith in the myth is tested by harsh realities which he alternately faces and flees. He fights to hold on to his identity. This means holding on to his faith, and, in the name of faith, Willy lies constantly: about the gross sales he has made, about the reaction of businessmen to his personality, about his boys' success and importance, about his own prospects. These lies echo, not the drab reality about him, but the shining hope he has. From the observer's point of view established in the play through Charley and Linda, they are pathetic efforts to protect his identity. Willy is unfaithful to his long-suffering wife, but this infidelity is an assuagement of his loneliness on the road, a restorative to his flagging spirits, and a provision against the rebuffs of the day. When he momentarily faces reality—his inability to drive to Boston, the mounting bills and the dwindling income—he has to flee to the past and to project the future. The salesman cannot abandon the myth without reducing himself to zero. Thus he must hope.

CHAPTER 3

Relationships in *Death of a Salesman*

Characters in *Death of a Salesman*

Bernard F. Dukore

Bernard F. Dukore writes that each member of the Loman family is struggling to find meaning in an impersonal, urbanized world. He suggests that Willy is alienated, distracted by daydreams and plagued by contradictions. Willy's confused values condemn him to live in a distorted, insecure reality that is defined by a profound sense of meaninglessness. Biff blames his own failure on his father. Although Biff rebuffs Willy, he still seeks his father's approval. By the end of the play, Biff, unlike Willy, realizes that his empty values are the cause of his frustration and low self-esteem. Happy, on the other hand, fails to learn from his father's misplaced values. Like Willy, Happy brags about his accomplishments, links happiness to money, and overemphasizes the need to be liked. Suffering from the fact that he is the less favored son, Happy can't commit to anything and, despite having many women, feels alienated and lonely. Linda is not overly passive and dense as many critics assert. Instead, her reality is uncomplicated and she has the capacity to love and affirm, providing Willy some sense of stature and humanity as a man.

Bernard F. Dukore is a professor of theater arts and humanities at Virginia Polytechnic Institute. He has written extensively about the theater, playwrights, and dramatic theory and criticism.

Each week, Willy is on the road for five days. With more than 70 per cent of his time away from his family, he focuses on his work and the values associated with it, but his infidelities disturb him profoundly (Linda seems unaware of them). Characters he remembers personify his aims. Like

Ben, he wants to succeed in business. Like his father, who made flutes, he makes things with his hands, and he brags to Charley of the ceiling he put up. Like the legendary Dave Singleman, he wants to be well liked. To be well liked, he tries like the stereotypical salesman of popular mythology to amuse people with risqué jokes. In the remembered past, he slaps the Woman in Boston's fanny and exclaims, 'bottoms up!' In time present, he asks Charley's secretary, 'How're ya? Workin'? Or still honest?'

A failure in his work, he fears the present and romanticises the past, to which his mind continually reverts. But he fears the past as well—which may be why he romanticises it. Whereas at the start of the play he recalls a happy time on the road, at the end he recalls a traumatic experience there. Alienated from his beloved older son, he is also alienated from the world around him and from his past. His first appearance is an image of alienation: a solitary figure, dwarfed by his surroundings, weighed down by his actual and emotional luggage. Setting the tone of the play, this initial view defines Willy negatively, not by what he did but by what he did not do. His statement that nothing happened to make him return prematurely from his sales trip means he was not in an auto accident. The nothing that happened was an inability to drive beyond a northern suburb of New York City.

His daydreams while driving were occasioned by the beautiful scenery he passed—a striking contrast to the ugly apartment buildings surrounding his house. Such contrast or contradiction is a frequent characterising device. Although Willy claims identity as the firm's New England man, he complains that he is not in the New York office. He says the Chevrolet is the greatest car ever made but repairs are so expensive its manufacture should be prohibited. After he twice condemns Biff for laziness, he admiringly says the boy is not lazy. Exclaiming that Biff's not finding himself at age 34 is disgraceful, he soon announces that some eminent men do not get started until later in life. He calls himself well liked but admits that people do not take to him. He first declares that a man should have few words, next that since life is short some jokes are in order, then that he jokes too much. His speech reflects his conflicting values and lack of control. When a complaint about the encroaching apartment buildings is succeeded by one about his salesmanship ('Population is getting out of control. The competition is maddening!'), he reveals the latter to be his real fear—ironic, since a salesman should welcome many potential customers.

One ought not to accept Willy's statements at face value. Whether he recalls his father (whom he last saw when he was four), Ben (whom he barely knew) or Dave Singleman, we cannot accept his say-so or (with Ben) the projection of his think-so. He so frequently distorts reality, we can be sure that he does not fully comprehend himself or society. From a statement that Father Wagner asked him what he thought of the name Howard for his son, he leaps to 'I named him Howard'. His counsel to Biff on how to conduct himself in a business interview reverberates on himself. He advises Biff to be serious, not to say boy's words like 'Gee', be modest or look worried. Instead, he should begin with a few jokes, for personality will win the day. 'And if anything falls off the desk while you're talking to him—like a package or something—don't you pick it up. They have office boys for that.' The contradiction between advice to be serious and to tell jokes alerts us to notice that Willy does not follow his own guidance. His final speech in Act I starts 'Gee', which he repeats soon after Act II begins and uses again when he enters the restaurant. When he sees his employer, Willy is worried and modest, if not subservient. At one point, Howard '*looks for his lighter. Willy has picked it up and gives it to him.*'

Miller's portrait of Willy Loman is more subtle than one may first realise. He wants his sons to succeed more spectacularly than anyone else and is ashamed that they have not done so. Upon learning of the adult Bernard's success, Willy is '*shocked, pained*', but also '*happy*'. To ask Bernard, whom he had despised as puny, the secret of his success and Biff's failure requires a great effort; but Willy makes the effort. Although he loves his wife, he subconsciously blames her for his failure. If he had gone to Alaska with Ben when he had the chance to do so, he laments, his life would have been different. Apart from the dubiousness of whether a tycoon would have said to Willy, at 46 and with no experience of managing a business, 'I need a man to look after things for me. . . . Screw on your fists and you can fight for a fortune up there', Willy's hallucination has Linda '*frightened of Ben and angry at him*', arguing that Willy has a good job, is well liked and will some day be made a member of the firm. Furthermore, as John Elsom observes: 'We do not learn about Loman's dilemmas through Loman's eyes, because we always know more about his failure than he does'. An 'object lesson', Willy 'is not discovering hard realities on our behalf'. In contrast to *A View from the Bridge*, no *raisonneur* tells us about him.

Miller calls Willy a true believer, a zealot. If he did not have 'a very profound sense that his life as lived had left him hollow, he would have died very contentedly polishing his car on some Sunday morning at a ripe old age'. Because he cannot realise the ideals to which he is intensely dedicated, he feels frantic. He seeks 'a kind of ecstasy in life which the machine civilization deprives people of. He is looking for his selfhood, for his immortal soul, so to speak'.

As Neil Carson[1] points out, Willy is a son as well as a father. Insecure from childhood, when his father abandoned the family, he has always felt 'kind of temporary' about himself. Thus, he is overly supportive of his older son. When Biff fails math, Willy blames the teacher. Thus too, he excessively adores the boy. 'If young Biff steals it is courage. If he captains a football team, the world is watching'. In emulating Dave Singleman by choosing his profession, Willy hopes to gain what Singleman possesses, love, which is what he demands from his son. Beyond the contrast to urbanization, the garden suggests that Willy's seeds cannot take root or develop. Failing with garden and sons, Willy in the final act tries to plant seeds at night using a flashlight—an image that combines family, home and society.

THE CHARACTER OF BIFF

Among the play's polarities are the family and the jungle, domestic security and the dangerous world of business. Willy's father and brother chose the latter, and while Ben had a wife and seven sons, his primary identification is with business, which he calls a jungle. Willy is drawn to both poles. Devoted to his family, he regards society as a jungle with burning woods, predatory animals and competitors trying to beat him to the spoils. Neither of his sons marries or fosters a family—that is, neither emulates him. Biff's actions parody adventurousness and business enterprise: punching cattle and petty theft. Replacing marriage with one-night stands, Happy like Willy does not leave home.

Despite Biff's rejection of his father after their encounter

---

1. literary critic

in Boston, Willy's ways are imprinted in him. In the restaurant, he mimics his father's line of patter. When Letta asks whether he was ever on a jury, he quips, 'No, but I been in front of them'. The hotel scene, says Carson, gives him a shock of sufficient force that he cannot perceive the truth about himself for seventeen years. 'His anger with his father serves as an excuse to avoid looking for the real causes of his failure which are in himself.' As if to demonstrate the worthlessness of his father's real values (as he discovered them in Boston), Biff carries one such value to an extreme: encouraged to 'get away with' thievery when a boy (stealing lumber), he continues stealing as an adult, as if to demonstrate how wrong his father was. Furthermore, Biff refuses to do what his father hopes he will do: complete his studies, attend a university and succeed at business. Yet he continues to seek parental approval as a man. He does not know what he wants but what he is supposed to want, and he becomes particularly dissatisfied with his life out West in the spring (the anniversary of his discovery of his father's adultery). Losing confidence in his father, he loses confidence in himself (with women as well as in business). Verbally connecting his father and himself, his plea 'help him' turns in the next breath to 'help me'. Whereas both have business interviews, only Biff gains self-knowledge as a result. His new recognition consists of embracing an aspect of Willy that Willy rejects as a worthwhile career goal: an uncompetitive life in the outdoors.

Biff's recognition that he and his father are 'a dime a dozen' conflicts with his father's insistence that each is a unique individual. Miller regrets that Biff's perception, designed to provide uplift, does not more adequately counterbalance Willy's disaster. Fortunately, he has not revised the play to strengthen it, since it might then become an italicised message.

Willy's charge that Biff ruined his life because Biff blames him is accurate—as Biff inadvertently concedes: 'I never got anywhere because you blew me so full of hot air, I could never stand taking orders from anybody! That's whose fault it is!' To insist 'I'm nothing' is to deny Willy's hopes that he would be everything, and to urge Willy to admit the same is as vengeful as Willy claims. By saying 'There's no spite in it any more', Biff tacitly admits there once was.

Critics who complain that Biff's new vision diminishes

horizons, is a joyless recognition of failure, and is vague, trite and romantic, miss the point. Through Biff, Miller presents a nonidealistic understanding that for people like him ideals bring frustration, failure and loss of self-esteem. While the myth of the last frontier may have diminished from Alaskan horizons to the New England territory to a ranch, the last brings greater satisfaction to Biff than urbanised drudgery.

Nevertheless, Biff's self-recognition conveys a sense of loss. However commendable Biff's preparedness to leave may be, Willy's commitment to his sons and his determination to hope and fight may be a more uplifting vision—despite its futility. The dichotomy provides tension and complexity.

THE CHARACTER OF HAPPY

On one level, Happy understands his father: a poor salesman, he is 'sometimes . . . a sweet personality'. On another, he fails to learn from his father's mistaken values. 'He fought it out here' echoes Willy's 'We'll do it here, Ben!' The younger, less-favoured son tries harder than the older to be like, therefore loved by, the father. He claims to want a girl just like the girl who married dear old dad—one who would resist a hustler like himself—but since he says, using a cliché as his father would, 'They broke the mould when they made her', he does not seek a woman with her qualities. Like his father, he bloats his professional achievements; and he condemns Biff because he cannot earn much money out West. Recycling his father's liked/well liked antithesis, he encourages Miss Forsythe to disengage herself for the evening: 'Don't try, honey, try hard'. Like his father's brags, his should not be accepted at face value. Would a man who built a magnificent estate on Long Island be a good friend of a person like Happy? Because the man lived in it for two months, then sold it to build another, Happy concludes, he cannot enjoy it once it has been finished; but his conclusion may reflect his incomprehension: the man may have built it to sell at a profit. Is Happy so influential that manufacturers offer him hundred dollar bribes (equal to about six hundred today) to throw business their way?

Like Willy, Happy is alienated. Despite a profusion of women (the pick-up we see makes that boast credible), he calls himself lonely. Unwilling to commit himself, he keeps 'knockin' them over and it doesn't mean anything'. While this statement anticipates Willy's, that the Woman in Boston means nothing, differences are more striking: Willy talks of one woman (the only affair we know of), he offers a humane explanation and his emotional commitment to Linda is real. Without a family to sustain him, Happy is a deterioration from his father. Like Willy, Happy wants to succeed at business. But his imagery debases religion to monetary terms: when the marketing manager enters the store 'the waves part in front of him' and unlike the spiritual aura exuded by Moses when he led the Israelites across the Red Sea, the aura surrounding the manager consists of 52 000 dollars a year.

Both Willy and Linda define Happy's status as less-favoured younger son. After Biff tells Willy of the football he 'borrowed':

WILLY: (*laughing with him at the theft*) I want you to return that.

HAPPY: I told you he wouldn't like it.

BIFF: (*angrily*) Well, I'm bringing it back!

WILLY: (*stopping the incipient argument, to Happy*) Sure, he's gotta practise with a regulation ball, doesn't he? (*To Biff*) Coach'll probably congratulate you on your initiative!

Willy sides with the older son against the younger. In time present, he and his wife do the same when Happy seeks their approbation and notice. In Act I, after Willy reiterates that Biff has greatness in him and Linda cries to her darling to sleep well, the ignored younger brother calls for approval: 'I'm gonna get married, Mom'. Her response: 'Go to sleep, dear'. His father's: 'Keep up the good work'. Although Linda demands attention for Willy, she gives none to Happy, whom Willy also ignores. In Act II, Happy puts his arm around his mother and addresses his father: 'I'm getting married, Pop, don't forget it. I'm changing everything. I'm gonna run that department before the year is up'. Willy turns away from him. Small wonder, then, that Happy fails to respond to Biff's charges that he does nothing for their father, who means nothing to him. The neglected son has his revenge. Ushering Miss Forsythe out of the restaurant, he interrupts her suggestion that he tell his father he is leaving: 'No, that's not my father. He's just a guy'. More basically, he revenges himself on his father and brother through philandering. By refusing to marry, he rejects his father's value system; to prove he is more of a man than his brother, an athletic hero, he excels in the sexual arena.

THE CHARACTER OF LINDA

Willy calls Linda his foundation and support. She tries to make the boys treat him decently and encourages him when he needs reassurance. She is neither stupid nor overly passive, as some assert. Were she to nag Willy to face reality, he might emulate his father and abandon the family; and critics might condemn her for the zealotry of Gregers Werle in *The Wild Duck.*[2] Not as deluded about reality as Willy is, she wonders whether Bill Oliver will remember Biff; and she is far from a doormat when her sons fail their duties to their father.

Miller most fully reveals Linda in three scenes from which Willy is absent. In the first, she primarily pleads his case as a man. Although he never earned much money or was the most wonderful person in the world, he is a human being in crisis, to whom attention should be paid. A small person can be as exhausted as a great one, and while his business associates do not accord him recognition, neither do his sons, for whose benefit he worked. Perhaps the most famous speech in the play, it defines Willy and gives him stature. In the second scene, primarily pleading his case as a father, she castigates her sons for having deserted him as they would not have a stranger. In the third, she eulogises a husband she loves. Far from demonstrating stupidity, her incomprehension of why he committed suicide derives from what she, not the audience, was aware of. When she last saw Willy, he was happy because Biff loved him. These three scenes provide a more rounded view of Willy and Linda than we might otherwise receive.

2. Play by Norwegian playwright, Henrik Ibsen

Sexual Relationships in *Death of a Salesman*

Ronald Hayman

Ronald Hayman argues that Miller uses Willy's, Happy's, and Biff's dysfunctional sexual relationships to reflect their social conditioning and their resentment of the roles that society forces them to play. Willy, for example, unable to bond sincerely and honestly with Linda, attempts to "sell" himself to her, but she is not fooled by his boasting and bloated self-importance. Willy turns to superficial sexual infidelities with other women where he can inflate his self-image with wisecracks and slick sales talk. Hayman writes that both Happy and Biff share Willy's inability to connect meaningfully with women. In the restaurant scene, the Loman brothers employ the same sales-talk banter to seduce the two girls that Willy used in Boston with The Woman.

Ronald Hayman is a contributor to the Frederick Ungar World Dramatists Series. He has written other critical books on authors Edward Albee, Arthur Miller, and John Osborne.

Eric Bentley[1] has suggested that the use of sex serves to mask the social criticism in the play and to offer an alternative explanation of the disasters that befall the protagonists. I would say, on the contrary, that all through the play Miller uses sex as a means of carrying his social argument forward. Willy, Biff, and Happy all behave badly over sexual relationships and in each case Miller demonstrates very effectively how the bad behavior both reflects their social conditioning and expresses their resentment of the role society forces them to play.

The failure of Willy's relationship with Linda is closely linked to his failure as a salesman. He believes, wrongly,

1. American literary critic

that he needs to sell himself to her, to impress her by big talk. Even at the time he was doing relatively well, he was barely able to keep ahead of their time-payment commitments, but he always talked as though he were doing better than he really was. In spite of her love, she was never able to convince him that he was good enough for her as he actually was, in himself, and it was partly his failure to impress her as much as he felt she needed to be impressed that drove him into the arms of other women. To them he could boast without having his bluff called. So he sold himself to them with wisecracks and gifts of silk stockings.

Happy, who like Biff has been blown "full of hot air" by Willy all through his childhood, knows that he can outbox, outrun, and outlift anyone in the store. He resents having to work under men who are physically his inferiors and he revenges himself by seducing their fiancées.

> Sure, the guy's in line for the vice-presidency of the store. I don't know what gets into me, maybe I just have an overdeveloped sense of competition or something, but I went and ruined her, and furthermore I can't get rid of her. And he's the third executive I've done that to. Isn't that a crummy characteristic? And to top it all, I go to their weddings!

The two major sequences involving sex are Willy's affair with The Woman and the boys' episode with the two girls in the restaurant. Willy's affair is in the past but it gets brought powerfully into the present, particularly during the restaurant scene.

WILLY'S INFIDELITY

The importance of the infidelity to Linda is judged mainly in terms of the effect it has on Biff. This is shown very skillfully. Bernard, when he meets Willy in his father's office, is curious to know what it was that stopped Biff from trying to qualify for a university. At school he failed only one subject and he could have made this up by going to summer school. Bernard knows that something happened in Boston, where Biff went to visit Willy, which was a turning point in his life, for afterward he adamantly refused to enroll for summer school. We do not find out what it was that happened until after we have seen Biff and Happy in action with the two girls. Happy's way of sweetening them up is a simple application of the principles of salesmanship. He gets into conversation with the first girl by pretending to be a champagne salesman and telling the co-operative waiter to bring her a bottle of what he says is his brand. On Biff's arrival, Happy persuades her to ask a girl friend to come along by selling Biff to her as a great football player. His conversation is full of sales-talky wisecracks.

When Willy arrives at the restaurant, he has just been fired and, as in the earlier scene with Charley, he is living partly in the past. Interspersed through his conversation with the boys are lines that flash him (and us) back to the hotel in Boston. The Woman is first heard laughing off-stage and then heard speaking lines from off-stage, but we do not see her until after Willy has hit Biff and after Biff and Happy have gone off with the two girls.

In actuality Willy is now in the washroom of the restaurant; in his mind he is in the Boston-hotel bedroom with The Woman. The knocking on the door is both nightmarish and expressive of guilt, like the knocking after the murder in *Macbeth*. Willy first denies that there is any knocking and when he finally has to open the door, it is Biff. By now, Willy has hidden The Woman in the bathroom and he has every chance of getting rid of Biff before she comes out, but characteristically, after telling him to go and wait downstairs, in his giggling admiration of the boy, he encourages him to repeat an imitation he has done of a schoolmaster. When The Woman starts laughing in the bathroom and comes out half-naked, nothing Willy says or does can help. The experience is traumatic for Biff—just as if he were much younger than he actually is. The jerk back into the present tense leaves Willy on his knees in the washroom.

It is ironical and touching that immediately after this re-enactment of Willy's infidelity, we see Linda's loyalty to him in the implacable scorn she shows toward her two sons after their behavior to Willy in the restaurant. Biff's climacteric argument with Willy is far better written than the final scene between Chris and Joe in *All My Sons*. The language is straightforward, but unlike the more ambitious language of *All My Sons* it is adequate to the situation, which in the theater creates enough tension to pull the dialogue very taut:

BIFF: I stole myself out of every good job since high school!

WILLY: And whose fault is that?

BIFF: And I never got anywhere because you blew me so full of hot air I could never stand taking orders from anybody! That's whose fault it is!

WILLY: I hear that!

LINDA: Don't, Biff!

BIFF: It's goddam time you heard that! I had to be boss big shot in two weeks, and I'm through with it!

WILLY: Then hang yourself! For spite, hang yourself!

BIFF: No! Nobody's hanging himself, Willy! I ran down eleven flights with a pen in my hand today. And suddenly I stopped, you hear me? And in the middle of that office building, do you hear this? I stopped in the middle of that building and I saw— the sky. I saw the things that I love in this world. The work and the food and time to sit and smoke. And I looked at the pen and said to myself, what the hell am I grabbing this for? Why am I trying to become what I don't want to be? What am I doing in an office, making a contemptuous, begging fool of myself, when all I want is out there, waiting for me the minute I say I know who I am! Why can't I say that, Willy? [*He tries to make Willy face him, but Willy pulls away and moves to the left.*]

WILLY [*with hatred, threateningly*]: The door of your life is wide open!

BIFF: Pop! I'm a dime a dozen, and so are you!

WILLY [*turning on him now in an uncontrolled outburst*]: I am not a dime a dozen! I am Willy Loman, and you are Biff Loman!

[*Biff starts for Willy, but is blocked by Happy. In his fury, Biff seems on the verge of attacking his father.*]

BIFF: I am not a leader of men, Willy, and neither are you. You were never anything but a hardworking drummer who landed in the ash can like all the rest of them! I'm one dollar an hour, Willy! I tried seven states and couldn't raise it. A buck an hour! Do you gather my meaning? I'm not bringing home any prizes any more, and you're going to stop waiting for me to bring them home!

WILLY [*directly to Biff*]: You vengeful, spiteful mutt! [*Biff breaks from Happy. Willy, in fright, starts up the stairs. Biff grabs him.*]

BIFF [*at the peak of his fury*]: Pop, I'm nothing! I'm nothing, Pop. Can't you understand that? There's no spite in it any more. I'm just what I am, that's all.[*Biff's fury has spent itself, and he breaks down, sobbing, holding on to Willy, who dumbly fumbles for Biff's face.*]

WILLY [*astonished*]: What're you doing? What're you doing? [*To Linda.*] Why is he crying?

BIFF [*crying, broken*]: Will you let me go, for Christ's sake? Will you take that phony dream and burn it before something happens? [*Struggling to contain himself, he pulls away and moves to the stairs.*] I'll go in the morning. Put him—put him to bed. [*Exhausted, Biff moves up the stairs to his room.*]

WILLY [*after a long pause, astonished, elevated*]: Isn't that—isn't that remarkable? Biff—he likes me!

THE MEANING OF WILLY'S DEATH

It is worth quoting Arthur Miller's explanation of how Willy is driven to his death by this revelation of love:

> In this he is given his existence, so to speak—his fatherhood, for which he has always striven and which until now he could not achieve. That he is unable to take victory thoroughly to his heart, that it closes the circle for him and propels him to his death, is the wage of his sin, which was to have committed himself so completely to the counterfeits of dignity and the false coinage embodied in his idea of success that he can prove his existence only by bestowing "power" on his posterity, a power deriving from the sale of his last asset, himself, for the price of his insurance policy.
>
> I must confess here to a miscalculation, however . . . I did not realize either how few would be impressed by the fact that this man is actually a very brave spirit who cannot settle for half but must pursue his dream of himself to the end. . . . Had Willy been unaware of his separation from values that endure he would have died contentedly while polishing his car, probably on a Sunday afternoon with the ball game coming over the radio. But he was agonized by his awareness of being in a false position, so constantly haunted by the hollowness of all he had placed his faith in, so aware, in short, that he must somehow be filled in his spirit or fly apart, that he staked his very life on the ultimate assertion.

This analysis of what it is that makes Willy into an effective tragic hero also has its bearing on John Proctor in *The Crucible* and Eddie Carbone in *A View from the Bridge*, who are also brave and also unable to "settle for half."

But Willy is different in that his death is both something with a cash value and an idea that he has to sell himself. Altogether the selling in the play proves to be a much more useful dramatic currency than the "pipe dreams" in [American playwright] Eugene O'Neill's *The Iceman Cometh*, to which it is roughly comparable. But in *Death of a Salesman*, the words are always far more closely welded to action.

Women in *Death of a Salesman*

Kay Stanton

Kay Stanton suggests that in *Death of A Salesman,* women are subjugated and exploited. In the business world women are relegated to handling details that men feel are too trivial for masculine attention. Stanton argues that male success is also linked to the sexual exploitation of women. Biff's self-confidence, for example, is tied directly to his sexual self-confidence. Happy exploits women by using them as markers of his own power. If he can't beat his male competitors, he can lash out at them by triumphing sexually over their women.

According to Stanton, Linda is subjugated in Willy's home. Despite the fact that she is more astute and psychologically sound than Willy, she is placed in an inferior position and is expected to express unwavering support for her husband. Ironically, only Linda has a sense of what is valuable, the men don't.

Kay Stanton is an associate professor of English at California State University at Fullerton. She has published numerous articles on writers and she is the author of a feminist sequel to Miller's play entitled *Death of a Salesman's Wife.*

Arthur Miller's stated intention for *Death of a Salesman* was to create a "tragedy of the common man." Although commentators argue over the meaning of "tragedy" in this phrase, the word "man" has been taken as sexually specific rather than as generic in most responses to the play. Undoubtedly, the play is heavily masculine. Willy Loman is the tragic protagonist, and the effects of his tragic flaws are clearly engraved upon his sons. The roots of Willy's tragedy seem to be in his lack of attention from his father and his perceived in-

Reprinted from Kay Stanton, "Women and the American Dream of *Death of a Salesman*," in *Feminist Rereadings of Modern American Drama,* edited by June Schlueter (Rutherford, NJ: Fairleigh Dickinson University Press, 1989). Used by permission of Associated University Presses, © 1989.

adequacy to his brother, Ben. All conflicts seem to be male-male—Willy versus Biff, Willy versus Howard, Willy versus Charley—so it has been easy for productions, audiences, and commentators to overlook, patronize, or devalue the significance of women in the play. The tragedy of Willy Loman, however, is also the tragedy of American society's pursuit of the American Dream, which the play both defines and criticizes. Careful analysis reveals that the American Dream as presented in *Death of a Salesman* is male-oriented, but it requires unacknowledged dependence upon women as well as women's subjugation and exploitation.

The masculine mythos of the American Dream as personified in Willy Loman has three competing dimensions: the Green World, the Business World, and the Home. All three have ascendant male figure heads and submerged female presences. . . .

WOMEN IN THE BUSINESS WORLD

The myth of the American Business World provides Willy with the fantasy means of beating his father and his brother. But the complexity of the Business World also defeats the simplicity of the Green World. Ben proudly claims to have had many enterprises and never kept books, but such practices are impossible in the Business World. Decision-making and increased competition take the place of handcrafting and manual exploitation of resources. Yet women are the submerged element in this realm, too. As the male realm moves indoors, it brings in the female to attend to the details of daily maintenance considered too trivial for male attention—typing letters, keeping records, collecting evidence, and, perhaps the most important function, screening out lesser men. Instead of testing himself directly on feminine nature, a man in the Business World must test himself by making an important impression on the female secretary-receptionist before meeting with the male decision-maker. Thus the female provides access to the patriarchal male authority. This element is seen clearly in Biff's attempt to make a date with Bill Oliver's secretary to gain access to him, after waiting five hours unsuccessfully, and in The Woman's statement that Willy has "ruined" her because, after their sexual liaison, she now sends him directly to the buyers, without waiting at her desk. . . .

Women in the Business World are marked as whores simply because they are there, perhaps because of their function as access givers, although the reconstitution of the submerged shows them to be otherwise. As Willy, deeply and loudly involved in one of his flashbacks, approaches Charley's office to borrow money, Jenny, Charley's secretary, tells Bernard that Willy is arguing with nobody and that she has a lot of typing to do and cannot deal with Willy any more. She is an insightful, kind, put-upon, hard-working woman. When Willy sees her, he says, "How're ya? Workin'? Or still honest?", implying that her income is made through prostitution. To her polite reply, "Fine. How've you been feeling?", Willy again turns to sexual innuendo: "Not much any more, Jenny. Ha, ha!"

BIFF'S AND HAPPY'S EXPLOITATION OF WOMEN

Assertion of success for Biff, and especially for Happy, is also bound up with sexual exploitation of women. In their first appearance, they alternate between discussing their father and their own past and current lives, always coming to an association with women. When they recall their "dreams and plans" of the past, an immediate connection is made with "about five hundred women" who "would like to know what was said in this room." They hark back crudely to Happy's "first time," with "big Betsy something," a woman "on Bushwick Avenue," "With the collie dog": "there was a pig." Happy states that he "got less bashful" with women and Biff "got more so"; when he questions what happened to Biff's "old confidence", Biff returns the discussion to their father. Biff's self-confidence rests on sexual confidence; its diminishment is tied to his father. For Happy, success is measured using women as markers, as he moves up from the initial "pig" with a dog to "gorgeous creatures" that he can get "any time I want"—but to him they are still "creatures," not human beings like himself. Although Biff and Happy agree that they each should marry, find "a girl—steady, somebody with substance," "somebody . . . with resistance! Like Mom," Happy delights in turning other men's "Lindas" into his private objects of sport. He attributes his "overdeveloped sense of competition" to his habit of "ruining," deflowering, the fiancées of the executives at the store where he works, then attending their weddings to savor his secret triumph publicly. Because he cannot accept his low status in the Business World, he must take what he interprets to be the possessions of his superiors—their women—robbing them of their supposed only value, the gold of their virtue and jewels of their chastity, and delivering the damaged goods for his superiors to pay for over a lifetime of financial support. . . .

THE ROLE OF LINDA

The Home is the only realm where Willy can be the father, the patriarchal authority, so he invests it with sanctity. Much is made of the physical details of the Loman home in the opening stage directions. The home is *"small, fragile seeming,"* against a *"solid vault of apartment houses."* The house is symbolic of Willy, the apartment houses representative of the big uncaring society that has "boxed in" the little man. An *"air of the dream"* is said to cling to the Loman home, *"a dream arising out of reality."* We are given a few particulars of the reality: *"The kitchen at center seems actual enough,"* with its table, chairs, and the refrigerator, the palpability of which is underlined later through discussion of its repair needs. Other "real" elements are the brass bedstead and straight bedroom chair and *"a silver athletic trophy."* The set reflects Willy's mind, and these elements are most real in life to him. The kitchen and bedroom are the traditional areas of Woman and Linda, and the trophy is the one tangible piece of evidence of Willy's son Biff's "success."

The house evidently also represents the myth of the man's Home being his castle—or here, castle in the air, the *"air of the dream"* clinging to the Home. Willy's failure to get love from his father and brother in the Green World and his failures in the Business World can be obfuscated in the Home, where he is what he defines himself to be. In his interaction with his wife, Linda, Willy habitually patronizes, demeans, and expresses irritation at her; anything he says, no matter how trivial or self-contradictory, is made to seem more important than anything she says. Yet in one of his very few compliments to her, he says, "You're my foundation and my support, Linda." His praise of her is not only placed wholly in the context of himself, but it also partakes of architectural imagery, defining Linda's place in the Home. She is the foundation and support of the Home, the "real" element that Willy can extrapolate from and return to as he constructs his fantasy life.

The Loman men are all less than they hold themselves to be, but Linda is more than she is credited to be. She is indeed the foundation that has allowed the Loman men to build themselves up, if only in dreams, and she is the support that enables them to continue despite their failures. Linda is the one element holding the facade of the family together. Yet even Miller, her creator, seems not to have fully understood her character. Linda is described in the opening stage directions as follows: "*Most often jovial, she has developed an iron repression of her exceptions to Willy's behavior—she more than loves him, she admires him, as though his mercurial nature, his temper, his massive dreams and little cruelties, served her only as sharp reminders of the turbulent longings . . . which she shares but lacks the temperament to utter and follow to their end.*" She thus seems inferior to Willy; yet she demonstrates a level of education superior to his in terms of grammatical and mathematical ability, and she is definitely more gifted in diplomatic and psychological acumen. In her management of Willy, she embodies the American Dream ideal of the model post-World War II wife, infinitely supportive of her man. She makes no mistakes, has no flaws in wifely perfection. But the perfect American wife is not enough for American Dreamers like Willy. He has been unfaithful to her, and he rudely interrupts and silences her, even when she is merely expressing support for him. She can be the foundation of the house; he must rebuild the facade. . . .

Linda is the foundation and support not only of the Loman Home and Willy himself but also of the plea for sympathy for Willy of the play itself. She is used to establish Willy's significance as a human being to the boys and to the audience. In her most famous speech, she asserts that, although not a "great man," not rich or famous, and "not the finest character that ever lived," Willy is "a human being, and a terrible thing is happening to him. So attention must be paid. . . . Attention, attention must finally be paid to such a person." Linda thus articulates his value and notes the real worth beneath the sham presentation. But the boys have been taught too well by Willy to disregard her message. When she reveals that the company had taken Willy's salary away five weeks before, and Biff calls those responsible "ungrateful bastards," she states that they are no worse than his sons. The male world is ungrateful, unappreciative of such contributions as Willy made; only Linda understands and values them. Whenever she attempts to bring Biff and Happy to consideration for their father, they habitually shift blame away from themselves, pretend there is no problem, and/or change the subject and start bickering between themselves on their competing ideas and ideals. Just as

Willy leaves the repair of household appliances to Linda, the boys leave the repair of their broken-down father to her.

The Loman men do see Linda as a validator of value, but they objectify virtue in her and assume that, if they have a woman like her, they will possess virtue and not need to develop it on their own. Both Biff and Happy wish to marry a girl just like the girl who married dear old Dad, and they believe such possession will immediately transform their lives and bring them to maturity. They, like their father, want to subtract value from a woman to add to their own; none of the Loman men is able to keep an accurate account of himself. In the Loman Home, only Linda understands what has value, what things cost, and how much must be paid to maintain and repair the Home life. Her other function, therefore, is computing the family finances, doing the family math. She must tactfully bring Willy to face the truth of his commissions from his inflated exaggerations of success to maximize such resources as there are, and Willy resents her for returning him to the foundation of himself as lesser money-earner from his dreams of wealth. As representative and accountant of worth, she must be trivialized and devalued, as must math. . . .

THE ROLE OF THE WOMAN IN BOSTON

When Willy and Biff meet in Boston, both have failed: Biff has failed math, and Willy has failed marital fidelity. These failures are accompanied by masculine dream-value system failures: Willy has failed to uphold the family as the sacred cornerstone of success, and Biff has failed to be universally well liked by lesser men. In present time, each blames the other for his failure, but The Woman is made the foundation of the failed relationship between father and son. Although the Loman men contrast Linda as "somebody with resistance" with the women of the Business World, who can be "had," The Woman epitomizes those women, and she overlaps with and parallels Linda.

Willy continually links Linda and The Woman unconsciously. Linda's attempted ego-inflating praise of Willy in a flashback as the "handsomest man in the world" to her (after he had confessed feeling foolish to look at) brings on a flashback within a flashback in the laughter and then the first appearance of The Woman. Although in context the laughter signifies The Woman's enjoyment of Willy's company, the dramatic effect is that she is laughing at him rather than with him. As he comes out of the flashback within flashback to the flashback, Linda's laughter blends with that of The Woman. The Woman's laugh returns when evidence of Biff's bad behavior, provided by Linda and Bernard, haunts Willy's flashback, testifying that Willy raised Biff by the wrong standards—his rather than Linda's.

The Woman is not even dignified by a name in the list of characters and speech headings, although her name may be Miss Francis. By being simply The Woman, she figures as a temptress, a femme fatale, and this impression is reinforced by her laughter, the music accompanying her appearances, and her appearance in a black slip. Yet her description in the stage directions is at odds with this impression. She is *"quite proper-looking, Willy's age".* Furthermore, she is far from being a prostitute—she is a business contact of Willy's, someone (probably a secretary-receptionist) with the power to choose whom the buyers will see—and she lives with her sisters. Her payment for sex with Willy is silk stockings. She needs silk stockings to wear to work and can probably ill afford them on her salary. Yet the stockings also become an important symbol. When she mentions the promised stockings, Biff understands his father's relationship with her, and when Linda mends her own stockings, it reminds Willy of his guilt. Thus Linda and The Woman are bound together by the stockings, which reinforce their other connections: they are good-humored women of about the same age who both genuinely like Willy. The essential difference between them is that one has chosen to marry and work inside the Home, and the other has chosen not to marry and to work in the Business World. Linda herself is like a mended stocking, torn and tattered by Willy but still serviceable through the strengthening of her own moral fiber. The Woman is a "new" silk stocking, new territory on which Willy can test himself. Both are made to be objects, but both also witness the failures of masculine values.

Contrary to surface appearance, then, there are not two kinds of women in the play, good and bad. All of the women are conflated in the idea of Woman: all share more similarities than differences, particularly in their knowing, and having the potential to reveal, masculine inadequacy, although generally they have been socialized not to insult a man by revealing their knowledge to his face. The Loman men all agree that the truth of masculine inadequacy or failure must be kept from women, because if women do not know, men can maintain their pretenses among other men and to themselves. What most upsets Biff about his father's flashback ravings is that "Mom's hearing that!", and Happy habitually lies about himself and other men to women. When Willy borrows money from Charley, it is to pretend to Linda that it is his salary—but Linda knows about the loans. Willy tries to force Biff into a fabricated version of the meeting with Bill Oliver, supposedly so he can have good news to bring to Linda—but it is he, not Linda, who craves good news from Biff. Linda also knows and tells her sons that Willy has been trying to commit suicide. Like Letta, she is associated with collection and evaluation of evidence. Not only does Linda find the rubber gas hose (during her repairs), but she knows of other suicide attempts that Willy has made with the car. As she begins to tell the story of the witness, she says, "It seems there's a woman," and Biff quickly responds, "What woman?", obviously assuming that Linda means The Woman in Boston. Linda not only overlaps the function of Mother Loman, but she and the insurance company's woman witness are alike in knowing about Willy's suicide attempts; the woman witness is linked to The Woman in Biff's mind; Willy treats Jenny as he probably had treated The Woman; and, in the restaurant, Miss Forsythe and Letta provoke Willy's memory of The Woman, as had Linda. The synthesis that Willy seeks among the Green World, Business World, and Home is achieved not by male community but collectively through the women, who independently rise from their positions as submerged elements to join in a circle of femininity and summation of value that closes in, without acknowledgment, on the truth of the Loman men.

Biff and Willy

Sheila Huftel

Sheila Huftel writes that the lives of both Willy and
Biff fall apart when Biff catches his father with another woman in a Boston hotel room. Biff's life is defined by spite and a harsh rejection of Willy and his
definition of success. Willy, in turn, battles unsuccessfully to rehabilitate himself in Biff's eyes. Huftel argues that Willy ironically views his suicide as an affirmation, rather than a failure. In Willy's materialistic
world, he believes that he will bestow his last asset,
his life insurance policy, on a son who Willy finally
realizes truly loves him.

According to Huftel, Willy is victimized by modern
America's law of success that says anyone who fails at
business no longer belongs in society. In a sense, then,
Willy, a believer in the power of materialism, is forced
into an unwanted nonconformity outside society's definition of success.

Sheila Huftel was a drama critic for *The Stage*, a
British publication. Much of her material in *Arthur
Miller: The Burning Glass* came directly from inter-
views with Arthur Miller.

Let us get back to Willy, tormented by his situation; in particular, he cannot walk away from his relationship with his
son Biff, which broke down when Biff found his father with
a woman in a Boston hotel room. From that time he could
never see Willy as anything but "a phony little fake," and
never stopped trying to prove it. When Biff loses faith, so
does Willy. The disillusionment is brisk and brutal, not the
least of it being the humiliation of the woman; everything in
their lives falls after it. Willy spends the rest of his life trying
to rehabilitate himself in Biff's eyes, and Biff is lost. It is as
though he never grew beyond the seventeen-year-old who
flunked math. He defines himself to his brother Happy: "I'm

like a boy. I'm not married, I'm not in business, I just—I'm
like a boy." His life has stopped.

Willy cannot understand it: "Not finding yourself at the
age of thirty-four is a disgrace." Then, apart from Biff seeing
through Willy, he embodies a way of life that contradicts
Willy's standards of success; standards that Biff can neither
accept nor wholly reject. If Willy thinks Biff sees him only as
a fake, Biff is convinced that to Willy he is only a failure.

WILLY'S PREOCCUPATION WITH BIFF

For seventeen years Willy has been tearing himself apart over
this dead-end relationship. He cannot do anything about it. It
is elusive on the concrete, graspable level and he has nothing
to give Biff. Miller's classic situation, difficult enough to be
seen as impossible by everybody except Willy, who battles on
regardless. His position prompts the sane, practical advice to
leave things alone. He explains to Charley:

> WILLY: I can't understand it. He's going back to Texas again.
> What the hell is that?
>
> CHARLEY: Let him go.
>
> WILLY: I got nothin' to give him, Charley. I'm clean. I'm clean.
>
> CHARLEY: He won't starve. None of them starve. Forget about
> him.
>
> WILLY: Then what have I got to remember?
>
> CHARLEY: You take it too hard. To hell with it. When a deposit
> bottle is broken you don't get your nickel back.

Willy's preoccupation is just another thing that Charley will
never understand about him.

Willy, dragged along behind his dream, judges people by
the distance they are from attaining it. The most sudden
change is in his relationship with Bernard, Charley's son. It
moves from "You want him [Biff] to be a worm like Bernard?"
to seeing Bernard in his father's office, when he seems to re-
vere the boy he once despised. Bernard is on his way to argue
a case in the Supreme Court, and never mentions it to Willy.
Charley's forthright comment is: "He don't have to—he's
gonna do it." Miller's plays are full of these wry, perceptive,
and often brutal insights.

In his defeat Willy lives on the crowds cheering Biff the
day he captained the school football team. But now Biff
steals Oliver's fountain pen and to meet this crisis insists on
holding to facts; implacably he insists: "We've been talking
in a dream for fifteen years. I was a shipping clerk. . . . I was

never a salesman for Bill Oliver." They face it. It is a Miller play. And from this conflict of Biff's fact and Willy's dream the play moves toward Willy's inevitable suicide.

BIFF'S FAILURE

Death of a Salesman takes root deeper than Miller's other plays; for days, it seemed, I waited for Willy Loman to die. It's as though the play covers a life-span. You know the Lomans better than you do your neighbors. Just as there is no single, clear-cut reason for Biff's failure, there is no one reason for Willy's suicide. It would be gross oversimplification to suggest that one single action or event could explain a failure or prompt a suicide. Biff gave up his life out of spite, as Willy suggests. He failed because Willy brought him up to be a big shot and he could never take orders from anybody, as he himself admits. Equally, Biff could not give himself or his life to Willy's brand of success (as Miller sees) and by that standard he failed. All these are valid and contributing causes to Biff's failure; the answer does not lie in any one of them, and it is doubtful if the complete answer is to be found in all of them. Rightly, Biff's failure adds up to more than this and, rightly again, it cannot be completely explained. Once a character is fully created you can explain his actions no better or more satisfactorily than you can explain your own. In his Preface Miller warns: "A work of art is not handed down from Olympus from a creature with a vision as wide as the world."

WILLY'S SUICIDE

Let us go on to Willy's suicide, mercifully mixed in motive. "Revenge was in it and a power of love, a victory in that it would bequeath a fortune to the living and a flight from emptiness." But before Willy dies, Biff tries to show him how he had lived.

BIFF: Pop! I'm a dime a dozen, and so are you!

WILLY: I am not a dime a dozen! I am Willy Loman, and you are Biff Loman.

BIFF: I am not a leader of men, Willy, and neither are you. You were never anything but a hard-working drummer who landed in the ash can like the rest of them! I'm one dollar an hour, Willy! I tried in seven states and couldn't raise it. A buck an hour! Do you gather my meaning? I'm not bringing home any prizes any more, and you're going to stop waiting for me to bring them home! Pop, I'm nothing! I'm nothing,

Pop. Can't you understand that? There's no spite in it any more. I'm just what I am, that's all. . . . Will you let me go, for Christ's sake? Will you take that phony dream and burn it before something happens?

Willy's dream destroyed him and he died to turn it into reality. During his showdown with Biff, Willy hesitantly realizes that he is loved by his son; confirmed in his belief, he cries out his faith: "That boy—that boy is going to be magnificent."

Miller said of Willy in his Preface: "My sense of his character dictated his joy, and even what I felt was exaltation. In terms of his character, he had achieved a very powerful piece of knowledge, which is that he is loved by his son and has been embraced by him and forgiven. In this he is given his existence, so to speak—his fatherhood, for which he has always striven and which until now he could not achieve. That he is unable to take this victory thoroughly to his heart, that it closes the circle for him and propels him to his death, is the wage of his sin, which was to have committed himself so completely to the counterfeits of dignity and false coinage embodied in his idea of success that he can prove his existence only by bestowing 'power' on posterity, a power deriving from the sale of his last asset, himself, for the price of an insurance policy."

Willy's suicide remains affirmative in that, in his eyes, it resolves everything for him. He wins by his death all that he craved in life. Miller is convinced that the play is not a document of pessimism, and I do not think that it is.

Still following the dream of greatness, Willy imagines the size of his funeral. "They'll come from Maine, Massachusetts, Vermont, New Hampshire! . . . That boy will be thunderstruck." What an opportunity to dazzle Biff! But the funeral is attended only by the family, Charley, and Bernard. Willy dies as he has lived.

If this were the entire content of *Death of a Salesman* the play would be too personal to please Miller. *Salesman* has a greater depth and a wider vision, perhaps growing out of Miller's boyhood. As an adolescent during the second national catastrophe in American history—the Great Depression of the thirties, Miller learnt early to distrust success. In "Shadows of the Gods," writing of that time, he wondered whether success should be admired. "Or should one always see through it as an illusion which only existed to be blown up and its owner destroyed and humiliated?"

THE LAW OF SUCCESS AS A FORCE IN THE PLAY

Death of a Salesman is dominated by this law of success. It is the force behind the play and Miller writes chillingly about it in his Preface: "The confusion of some critics viewing *Death of a Salesman* . . . is that they do not see that Willy Loman has broken a law without whose protection life is insupportable if not incomprehensible to him and to many others; it is the law which says that a failure in society and in business has no right to live. Unlike the law against incest, the law of success is not administered by statute or church but it is very nearly as powerful in its grip upon men. The confusion increases because, while it is a law, it is by no means a wholly agreeable one even as it is slavishly obeyed, for to fail is no longer to belong to society in his estimate. Therefore, the path is opened for those who wish to call Willy merely a foolish man even as they themselves are living in obedience to the same law that killed him."

Unlike Miller's other characters, Willy desperately wants to conform to the way of life imposed upon him. A John Proctor,[1] for instance, does not believe with the majority, will not conform to it, and is sustained by the fact that he is right, but Willy's enforced nonconformity brings him only shame. His sense of right is vague at best and certainly no match for the pressures against him. Pressures that, incidentally, he cannot fight on the principle that you cannot fight what you would join. In these plays Willy is probably Miller's only nonconformist through circumstances, not choice. In this religion he would never dare to be a heretic.

The religion of success, like any other, has its myths, and Ben embodies legendary success. "William, when I walked into the jungle, I was seventeen. When I walked out I was twenty-one. And, by God, I was rich." This is exactly the way Willy would see success. Ben is Willy's older brother; he is also his daydream, the kind of man he wanted to become—his ideal image. In their dialogues, remembered or imagined, he is trying to achieve the viewpoint he has always sought, as well as confirmation of his own actions and beliefs. For Willy, it is an "ideal" conversation, one in which he is extending himself and, at the last, seeing himself as the practical, successful man he wanted to be. It is almost as though Miller wrote the character from a legendary angle;

1. Protagonist in Miller's *The Crucible*

fiction clings to Ben—fiction and a brutal realism that Willy could never reach: "Never fight fair with a stranger, boy. You'll never get out of the jungle that way."

Willy, on the other hand, puts all his faith in the individual, in the winning personality: "Be liked and you will never want" is the mainstream of his philosophy. The one line always remembered from *Salesman* is Willy's warning to his boys about Charley: "He's liked—but he's not well liked."

In Miller you always come back to the irrevocable fact, the unavoidable logic of a situation. "When a man gets old you fire him, you have to, he can't do the work." For these practical and impersonal reasons Willy was fired; his failure and the pain it causes him are pinned down to fact. As far as possible in Miller the intangible must be made tangible.

In Willy's sorry interview with Howard, he is too pushed and preoccupied with his own problems to choose his time; he interrupts Howard while he is absorbed in a wire recorder, a new toy he has bought for $150. Howard is fascinated by the machine and the breaking of the man goes unnoticed. He barely listens to Willy's plea: "You can't eat an orange and throw the peel away—a man is not a piece of fruit!" Undoubtedly Howard is bored with Willy, who seems to be doing no more than wasting his time. He has no use for him and sees him not as an individual but as an economic unit. One American critic saw this scene as party-line writing. Arthur Miller's name does not at once suggest politics to me, and the idea never entered my head. I believe that Miller's protest is directed toward the cutting down of the individual.

Death of a Salesman is of wide scope and great change covering Willy's life, but all that happens to Willy and Biff is implicit in it from the beginning. This dictates the audience's reaction of "Oh God, of course."

CHRONOLOGY

1914–1918

World War I

1915

Arthur Miller is born in New York City, the second of three children of Isidore and Augusta Barnett Miller; Arthur has an older brother, Kermit, and a younger sister, Joan, will be born in 1921

1917–1920

Russian Revolution

1921

Miller's sister, Joan, born

1928

Isidore Miller's business fails and the Miller family moves to Brooklyn

1929

The New York stock market crash and the start of the Great Depression

1933

Arthur graduates from high school to a number of odd jobs; while working as a shipping clerk, he discovers literature, including the influential Russian novel *The Brothers Karamazov* by Fyodor Dostoyevsky; President Franklin D. Roosevelt introduces New Deal reforms

1934

Miller enrolls at the University of Michigan

1936

Miller's first play, *No Villain*, wins University of Michigan's Avery Hopwood Award for drama

1937

Miller's play *They Too Arise*, a revised version of *No Villain*, earns a prize from the Theatre Guild Bureau of New Plays and his *Honors at Dawn* wins Avery Hopwood Award

1938

Miller graduates with a degree in English; moves back to New York and writes scripts for the Federal Theatre Project

1939–1945

World War II and the Holocaust

1940

Miller marries his college sweetheart, Mary Grace Slattery

1941

Japan bombs Pearl Harbor, December 7

1944

Miller's first child, Jane, is born; Miller tours army camps and writes a book of military reportage, *Situation Normal.* His first drama to play on Broadway, *The Man Who Had All the Luck*, closes after only six performances

1945

Miller's novel *Focus* is published; first atomic bomb is dropped on Hiroshima; Japanese surrender ends WWII in the Pacific

1947

Miller's second child, Robert, is born; after many drafts, Miller's play *All My Sons* is produced; 328 performances later, the play wins the New York Drama Critics' Circle Award

1949

Death of a Salesman opens in New York City; wins the Pulitzer Prize and the Antoinette Perry Award; Miller also publishes "Tragedy and the Common Man," the first of many essays on the nature of drama

1950–1953

Korean War

1950

Miller meets actress Marilyn Monroe; he writes an adaptation of Henrik Ibsen's play *An Enemy of the People*; McCarthyism and the Red Scare take hold in Washington

1953

The Crucible opens on Broadway

1955

Miller begins a relationship with Marilyn Monroe; writes *A View from the Bridge* and *A Memory of Two Mondays*

1956

Miller divorces Mary Slattery and marries Marilyn Monroe; he is subpoenaed to appear before the House Un-American Activities Committee (HUAC) and is cited for contempt of Congress; *A View from the Bridge* opens in London

1957

Miller's short story "The Misfits" appears in *Esquire* magazine; Miller also publishes *Collected Plays*; Soviet Union launches *Sputnik*, the first man-made satellite

1958

Miller's HUAC contempt conviction is reversed

1961

Miller's screenplay *The Misfits* is filmed starring Marilyn Monroe; Monroe and Miller divorce

1962

Miller marries photographer Inge Morath; Marilyn Monroe commits suicide; Cuban missile crisis

1963

President John Kennedy is assassinated in Dallas

1964

After the Fall opens in January and *Incident at Vichy* premieres in December; President Lyndon Johnson commits U.S. soldiers to the conflict in Vietnam

1965

Miller is elected president of the International Association of Poets, Playwrights, Editors, Essayists, and Novelists

1967

Miller publishes a collection of short stories, *I Don't Need You Anymore*

1968

The Price opens on Broadway; *Death of a Salesman* reaches sales of one million; Martin Luther King Jr. is assassinated in Memphis

1969

America lands a man on the moon

1970

Miller's works are banned in the Soviet Union as a result of his work to free dissident writers

1971

The Portable Arthur Miller is published

1972

The Creation of the World and Other Business opens and closes after twenty performances; Watergate scandal begins with burglary at Democratic Party national headquarters in Washington, D.C.

1974

Richard Nixon resigns U.S. presidency

1975

Miller works to free convicted murderer Peter Reilly; the last Americans are evacuated from Vietnam

1977

Miller petitions the Czech government to halt arrests of dissident writers; writes *The Archbishop's Ceiling*

1980

The American Clock premieres

1982

Miller writes two one-act plays, *Elegy for a Lady* and *Some Kind of Love*; Vietnam War memorial is unveiled in Washington, D.C.

1983

Miller and his wife travel to China to see a production of *Death of a Salesman* in Beijing

1984

Dustin Hoffman plays Willy Loman in a Broadway revival of *Death of a Salesman*; Ronald Reagan is elected to a second term as president

1985

Death of a Salesman airs on television to an audience of twenty-five million

1986

Miller writes *Danger: Memory!*

1987

Miller's autobiography, *Timebends: A Life*, is published

1990

Miller writes a screenplay for the motion picture *Everybody Wins*; President George Bush launches Operation Desert Storm against Iraq

1991

Miller's play *The Ride Down Mt. Morgan* opens in London; dissolution of the Soviet Union

1993

Miller's comedy-drama *The Last Yankee* premieres in New York

1996

Miller's screenplay of *The Crucible* is released

FOR FURTHER RESEARCH

BIOGRAPHICAL WORKS ABOUT AND INTERVIEWS WITH THE PLAYWRIGHT

Bernard Dekle, "Arthur Miller," in *Profiles of Modern American Authors*. Rutland, VT: Tuttle, 1969.

Bruce Glassman, *Arthur Miller*. Englewood Cliffs, NJ: Silver Burdett, 1990.

Jean Gould, "Arthur Miller," in *Modern American Playwrights*. New York: Dodd, Mead, 1966.

Elia Kazan, *Elia Kazan: A Life*. New York: Knopf, 1988.

Robert A. Martin and Steven R. Centola, *The Theater Essays of Arthur Miller*. New York: DaCapa Press, 1996.

Arthur Miller, *Salesman in Beijing*. New York: Viking Press, 1984.

Arthur Miller, *Timebends: A Life*. New York: Grove Press, 1987.

Benjamin Nelson, *Arthur Miller: Portrait of a Playwright*. New York: David McKay, 1970.

Matthew C. Roudané, ed., *Conversations with Arthur Miller*. Jackson: University Press of Mississippi, 1987.

ABOUT *DEATH OF A SALESMAN* AND MILLER'S PLAYS

Harold Bloom, ed., *Arthur Miller's* Death of a Salesman. New York: Chelsea House, 1988.

Harold Clurman, *Lies Like Truth*. New York: Simon & Schuster, 1958.

Robert Corrigan, ed., *Twentieth Century Views: Arthur Miller*. Englewood Cliffs, NJ: Prentice-Hall, 1969.

John H. Ferres, ed., *Twentieth Century Interpretations of* The Crucible. Englewood Cliffs, NJ: Prentice-Hall, 1992.

John D. Hurrell, *Two Modern American Tragedies: Reviews and Criticism of* Death of a Salesman *and* A Streetcar Named Desire. New York: Scribner's 1961.

Helen Wickham Koon, *Twentieth Century Interpretations of* Death of a Salesman: *A Collection of Critical Essays.* Englewood Cliffs, NJ: Prentice-Hall, 1983.

Robert A. Martin, ed., *Arthur Miller: New Perspectives.* Englewood Cliffs, NJ: Prentice-Hall, 1982.

Walter J. Merserve, ed., *The Merrill Studies in* Death of a Salesman. Columbus, OH: Charles E. Merrill, 1972.

Leonard Moss, *Arthur Miller.* Rev. ed. Boston: Twayne, 1980.

Brenda Murphy, *Miller:* Death of a Salesman. Cambridge: Cambridge University Press, 1995.

Benjamin Nelson, *Arthur Miller: Portrait of a Playwright.* London: Petrowen, 1970.

Gerald Weales, *American Drama Since World War II.* New York: Harcourt, Brace & World, 1962.

Sidney Howard White, *The Merrill Guide to Arthur Miller.* Columbus, OH: Charles E. Merrill, 1970.

HISTORICAL BACKGROUND

Thomas Adler, *American Drama, 1940–1960: A Critical History.* New York: Twayne, 1994.

Gerald M. Berkowitz, *American Drama of the Twentieth Century.* London: Longman, 1992.

C.W.E. Bigsby, *Modern American Drama, 1945–1990.* Cambridge: Cambridge University Press, 1992.

David Halberstam, *The Fifties.* New York: Fawcett Columbine, 1993.

Frederick Lumley, *Trends in Twentieth Century Drama.* New York: Oxford University Press, 1960.

George Jean Nathan, *Theatre in the Fifties.* New York: Knopf, 1953.

June Schlueter, *Feminist Rereadings of Modern American Drama.* Rutherford, NJ: Farleigh Dickinson University Press, 1989.

W. David Sievers, *Freud on Broadway: A History of Psychoanalysis and American Drama.* New York: Hermitage, 1955.

G.J. Watson, *Drama, An Introduction.* New York: St. Martin's, 1983.

WORKS BY ARTHUR MILLER

Arthur Miller's works are available in a wide variety of anthologies and reissues; therefore, facts of publication are omitted from the following list. All works are plays unless otherwise noted.

No Villain (1936)

Situation Normal (journal); *The Man Who Had All the Luck* (1944)

Focus (novel) (1945)

All My Sons (1947)

Death of a Salesman (1949)

Adaptation of Henrik Ibsen's *An Enemy of the People* (1950)

The Crucible (1953)

A View from the Bridge; *A Memory of Two Mondays* (1955)

Collected Plays (1957)

The Misfits (the screenplay) (1961)

After the Fall; *Incident at Vichy* (1964)

I Don't Need You Anymore (short stories) (1967)

The Price (1968)

The Creation of the World and Other Business (1972)

The Archbishop's Ceiling (1977)

The American Clock (1980)

Elegy for a Lady; *Some Kind of Love* (1982)

Danger: Memory! (1986)

Timebends: A Life (autobiography) (1987)

The Ride Down Mt. Morgan (1991)

The Last Yankee (1993)

INDEX